BUSINESS GOLF

BUSINESS GOLF

The Art of Building Relationships Through Golf

Pat Summerall

with

Will D. Rhame and James A. McNulty, CPA

A Birch Lane Press Book
Published by Carol Publishing Group

A Birch Lane Press Book
Published by Carol Publishing Group
Birch Lane Press is a registered trademark of Carol Communications, Inc.

Editorial, sales and distribution, and rights and permissions inquiries should
be addressed to Carol Publishing Group, 120 Enterprise Avenue, Secaucus,
N.J. 07094.

In Canada: Canadian Manda Group, One Atlantic Avenue, Suite 105, Toronto,
Ontario M6K 3E7

Carol Publishing Group books may be purchased in bulk at special discounts
for sales promotion, fund-raising, or educational purposes. Special editions
can be created to specifications. For details, contact Special Sales Department,
Carol Publishing Group, 120 Enterprise Avenue, Secaucus, N.J. 07094.

Manufactured in the United States of America
10   9   8   7   6   5   4   3   2   1

Library of Congress Cataloging-in-Publication Data

Summerall, Pat.
    Business golf :   the art of building relationships through golf /   Pat
    Summerall with Will D. Rhame and James A. McNulty.
            p.   cm.
    "A Birch Lane Press Book."
    Includes index.
    ISBN 1–55972–494–3 (hc)
    1. Success in business. 2. Strategic planning. 3. Business entertaining.
4. Public relations. 5. Golf—Psychological aspects. I. Rhame, Will D.
II. McNulty, James A. III. Title.
HF5386.S893   1999
658.4'095—dc21   98–48174
                                                                          CIP

Contents

Preface

This book is a joint effort to share, from the authors' personal experiences, validated through countless interviews with executives at all levels of industry, and across all levels of handicap, the secrets of building relationships through golf. It is dedicated to all those golfers who would like to use the game more productively as a tool for developing successful business relationships. Whether you are an accomplished golfer or a beginner, the insights, interviews, and techniques offered in *Business Golf* will help you understand your playing partners better, and in so doing you will learn to play the game of business with more confidence. The BusinessLinks premise is that we want to develop some relationship with golfers with whom we are spending time. We must learn to understand ourselves, our motives, personalities, habits, and strengths. But we can't ignore our weaknesses. We must want to improve our people skills, just as much as we want to improve our golf game. If there is potential to do business, it will more than likely make itself known. Certainly we have to go to the course with a healthy attitude about our objectives for the day. These are only a few assumptions we throw on the table, or the putting green, that are basic to understanding our views.

The first is that relationships are of the utmost importance to you in your business. The second is that you want to improve those relationships. The third is that you have a sense of humor or an appreciation for those whose normal demeanor may be less serious than your own. Finally, golf is an excellent venue to nurture relationships, and develop powerful personal bonds and long-lasting friendships. We believe that after reading *Business*

Golf, you will agree that your chances of enjoying and benefiting from the game will increase dramatically.

BusinessLinks (that's the term we'll use to mean a business golf experience) is a unique and structured concept that is different from competitive or social golf. There are specific rules, etiquette, and communication skills that must be understood to play it well. This book focuses on those skills, not the techniques of playing golf. We think that teaching the physical skills should be left to golf professionals, but we can't ignore the fact that the ability to have fun playing golf is directly related to how satisfied we are with the way we play the game. The more we enjoy playing, the more fun we will have.

Only 10 percent of golfers have less than an 18 handicap! Every golfer is capable of improving some part of his game. Tour professionals practice incessantly because they know they can improve. Club professionals do the same. John Updike calls golf a "narcotic pastime." No golfer ever "gets it perfect." We encourage you to increase your skill level with professional help, although most golfers are higher handicappers who are totally satisfied with their games. These golfers, too, can learn something from our findings, and they in turn will enjoy the game more.

Handicaps, theoretically, equalize all golfers. In Business-Links, having a handicap allows you to enjoy more of the relationship side of golf, like member-guest tournaments, scrambles, and occasional invitations to special courses around the world where it is expected that you can hold your own in a game, regardless of your handicap.

We want to improve the way the world plays golf by bringing to light the basic mistakes we all make, and in so doing, we want to educate all golfers—new and experienced alike—so the game will be more fun and productive for everyone. Incidentally, more business will be done as well, and the positive experiences around the game will skyrocket like a 280-yard power fade down a slight dogleg-right.

We purposely opted to identify by name only a few of the folks we talked to while writing this book. All of the stories are true, with the exception of a couple thrown in for laughs. Those who told us a story, or who were cordial enough to grant us an interview, will recognize their contributions. Pat Summerall's comments could fill a library, and we thank him for being part of our dream. We have included many excerpts from interviews with golfers from all walks of business, and those testimonies will show how to use golf as a tool to develop business relationships. We gratefully acknowledge all the contributions and thank our new friends for the insights they have shared with us.

Now, please join us in a round of BusinessLinks.

WILL D. RHAME AND JAMES A. McNULTY, CPA

Acknowledgments

Special thanks go to the following individuals whose invaluable support and encouragement led to the creativity resulting in this book: Wendell Conditt, Andy J. Kindle, Chuck Ruthe, Nick Arfaras, Molly O'Dea, Rick Odioso, Fred Ridley, Homer Hemingway, Tom Wilson, John Davidson, Gary Koch of the Professional Golf Association (PGA), Burt Linthicum, M. Katharine Post, Johnnie Jones (PGA), Penny White, Irv Thompson, William J. McNulty, Don Diehl, Renee McCollum, Dr. Richard T. Bowers, Dr. Paul J. Solomon, Hugh J. McNulty, Joseph Doyle, S. J., and Brady Fitzsimmons.

And there are others whose early influence and support for the coauthors created wonderful memories, on which we often reflect. They are: David P. Rhame, Denny Champagne (PGA), Pat Neal (PGA), Harold Rayborn (PGA), Dave Ragan (PGA), and Gil Gonsalves (PGA).

Introduction

Personal experience has taught me that golf can break down barriers between people and serve as a catalyst for a free exchange of ideas as well as a way of building lasting relationships. I have met people I didn't care for at first, but after playing with them, I discovered that they weren't bad people after all. I found that if I took the time to get to know others on a golf course, I would often view them in a different way. I have seen the good side as well as the competitive side of people, and each of us has a competitive side, though we may not show it. I think the fact that all players are equal on the golf course helps us bond both as friends and businessmen and -women. It doesn't make any difference how much ability we have, the handicap system works. It doesn't make any difference how much money we have, the handicap system still works. It is the great equalizer. Nor does it make any difference how many lessons we have had or even if we never took a lesson. According to the rules of golf and the way the game is played, we are all equal. You can marvel at your opponent's shots. He can do something just spectacular that you think you would only see on the PGA Tour, and at the same time you can make a thirty-foot putt that makes you feel just as good. Golf leaves us, at the end of the round, thinking, "Okay, I've done well today." If we only had this feeling about life.

PAT SUMMERALL

The BusinessLinks
Ten Commandments

1. Focus your attention on your guests, not your score.
2. Leave your ego in your bag.
3. Carefully choose all the members of your group.
4. Always arrive early and be prepared.
5. Play in a team format when appropriate.
6. Establish the rules before the first ball is hit.
7. Use "jitterfix" on the first tee when possible.
8. Keep a copy of the United States Golf Association (USGA) rule book in your bag.
9. Always "pick up" when appropriate.
10. Have a carefully planned follow-up procedure for every round of BusinessLinks.

Part I

THE BASICS OF BUSINESSLINKS

1

The Beginning of Business Golf

My success in business is due entirely to golf and, by the
way, I have a 20 handicap.

—CARPET MANUFACTURER'S REPRESENTATIVE

We will not go into the long history of golf as a sport. The
colorful characters who brought this game to us through
their awesome accomplishments, and those who continue to reward us with their masterful golf, are the subjects of
many books. An interested reader can find a plethora of material
on the history of the game. But, sadly, we found little on the subject of relationships built around the game.

We want to help more than thirty-five million golfers understand how golf was used early on as a relationship-building tool
and how it has evolved into today's $15-billion-dollar-a-year busi-
ness. Each year almost 480 million rounds of golf are played in
the United States alone! We want to teach golfers that it doesn't
matter if you are a 30-plus handicapper or a tour player. If you
know how to manage yourself effectively on the course, you can
easily and effectively play with players of all skill levels, either
for fun or to build business relationships.

David Hill on Golf and Lots of Business

I think it would be safe to say that many of the big deals in this
country are done on the golf course. I did my own deal to sign
with Fox television on the golf course playing with David Hill.
I've seen houses bought and sold, companies bought and sold,

3

*and I've seen golf used as a recruiting tool. I've seen a lot of deals
done through this game.*

Until recently, golf has been an elite social game, primarily
played by men. For years golf targeted the rich, the over forty,
and the retired businessperson. Ads and promotional propaganda
have offered the view that the true essence of success is having an
expensive car and the time to play golf several days a week.
Every employee familiar with the boss's habit of playing golf in
the middle of the week wonders how it is done. In fact, 98 percent of the Fortune 500 chief executive officers (CEOs) pick golf
as their sport of choice, and those CEOs encourage their top
employees to use the game to develop business relationships. It is
no wonder that so many people have taken up the game.

Golf has been referred to as the rich man's playground. Fortunately, that view is changing. Golf is much more accessible
now, thanks to a variety of reasons, including the availability of
more leisure time for all of us. How many real estate develop-
ments of any size are built with a golf community being touted as
an integral part of its lifestyle? Promotional literature flaunts the
good-looking young couple, or the happy retired couple, riding in
the golf cart down "Easy Street." Young children offer an ever-
increasing supply of new golfers all hungry to be the next young
star. Women are discovering the game by the thousands. Executive women are finding that they love this game, and their addition is making substantive changes in the stodgy rules many clubs
have lived by for generations. Couples are playing together.
Youngsters are enjoying more quality time with their parents and
grandparents. There is no better place to teach—or learn—people
skills. Even teenagers are having golf dates!

Several years ago, the Internal Revenue Service (IRS) rules
changed so that golf club membership expenses were no longer
deductible. Club owners and boards of directors were furious. To
those used to submitting golf expenditures for reimbursement, it
made a real economic difference. Prior to the changes, business-
people would entertain at the club and have their dues expensed
at the end of the year. Properly documented, entertainment at a
golf club was 100 percent deductible. When the IRS disallowed
the deductions, many experts thought it would signal the slow

demise of the private club and the end of golf as we knew it. Wrong! Certainly the restrictions on entertainment, and the disallowance of dues as a deductible cost made a difference in who pays the bill, but at least where we have made contacts, golf is booming. If the IRS commissioner would include golf as a requirement for all IRS employees, perhaps they wouldn't search so assiduously for the wrongly classified nondeductible expense on all those corporate audits.

A few large businesses started using golf as a part of their overall promotional budgets about forty years ago. Remember *The Wonderful World of Golf,* sponsored by Shell Oil Company? Quaker State, R.J. Reynolds Tobacco, and Cadillac grabbed the opportunity to advertise whenever they could. Shell Oil is now back in the game in a way they never considered as the founding partner of the World Golf Village (more on that project shortly). Big business and successful salespeople have recognized for years that you must be where the money is if you plan on making big sales. Only recently have smaller businesses been able to take advantage of golf as a means to promote the corporate agenda. The branding of corporate names through logoed gifts is a regular and effective way of reminding contacts and customers that the relationship is important. It is all part of the recruiting process, the sales call, and the follow-up thanks.

Public courses have sprung up throughout the country, which has made golf more accessible to anyone who wants to play, including those who can't afford, or choose not to join, a private club. The corporate arena has diversified to owning and managing public golf courses, because a properly managed and maintained public course is a moneymaker. In the sixties and seventies the "Big Four"—Arnold Palmer, Jack Nicklaus, Gary Player, and Tom Watson—helped create tremendous interest in the game, and now we have extensive television and cable coverage. We have a relatively new addition now with PGA Tour Radio. The professional men's and women's tours have exceptional television coverage all week long. Infomercials on golf products air at all hours of the day and night. Hollywood helped expose the game as a business sport with the introduction of the James Bond series.While golf has been used as a business tool since the building of old St. Andrews in Scotland, the baby boomers are credited with the discovery that golf can be a really powerful business-building tool.

Pat's Thoughts on How Golf Can Weave a Magic Spell

I think golf has a way of making people drop barriers as they wouldn't normally do in business. If we were in the office looking across a desk, one of us would be sitting in an advantageous position. The golf course equalizes us. Instead of sitting across the desk, you're competing with somebody on an equal footing. If we are asked what club to use or how far it is to the green, everyone seems to want to help everyone else. If somebody can't find the ball, everybody looks for it. It is all part of the process of getting to know each other, learning how we each conduct ourselves in a social atmosphere. If we can get along on a social basis and learn about our interests outside of the business setting, we are in a better position to arrange a business transaction. No matter how many bucks are involved, as long as we are sincere and genuine with each other, golf can weave a magic spell. Golf is different from any other situation. In tennis you are trying to beat somebody; in business you are trying to get something from the other party. In golf you are not trying to beat somebody per se, you are trying to beat the object, the ball, the scorecard, or the golf course. You are competing, but mainly against yourself, and your attitude is: What can I do in this battle with myself, how can I be better?

The Businessperson's Game

Golf has evolved into the businessperson's game. The National Golf Foundation estimates that two million new golfers will join the ranks annually. The numbers are staggering, and the average age and income that participates in golf is moving south fast. The statistics are wonderful! Everybody is enjoying the game. There is no excuse for anyone who wants to learn this game to not get started. All the tools, and all the venues, are reaching out to the new golfer. The National Golf Foundation reports that across the

Fred, you're always making fun of the fact I play golf.
Last month I brought in four new clients to your one!
Looks like you could use a lesson.

country the average cost of a game is now under $20. In every city of any size, municipal courses are available and affordable.

But let's go back to why golf has something of a stigma attached to it by such a large portion of would-be enthusiasts. The cost to play a round can vary from $15 to $250. Add the cost of equipment (from $100 to $5,000 or more), and we can easily believe that golfers in America spend on average $600 per year, and there are thirty-five million of us. Golf takes a lot of time. Typically, three and a half to four hours are needed to play eighteen holes. (If you take longer, you're too slow and should try to speed up, because you may be interfering with other golfers.)

It also takes a lot of time to learn how to play the game well. Playing well means knowing the rules and etiquette, when to allow a faster group to go through, or how to keep up with the group in front of you, and other subtle but important aspects of the game. If you have the gift of being a low handicapper, it means playing within your game, but making a higher handicapper feel comfortable when a poor shot is made. Golf can be quite intimidating, frustrating, mind-boggling, and yet very rewarding as well. With all the emphasis on using golf as a business tool, we want to help golfers of every skill level to get better at the people side of golf. It is estimated that nearly $2 billion are spent every year in nurturing and supporting business relationships around the game. Based on documented experience and countless interviews, we have determined that much of the money used for business relationships is wasted. Far too few people know how to communicate effectively, especially in business, and even fewer know how to communicate and manage themselves appropriately on the golf course. Yet we can't begin to calculate the amount of money that has been generated through new business relationships as a direct result of golf. We know of more than a few multimillion-dollar deals that have been consummated by individuals who attribute that transaction to a specific golf experience.

The Japanese Golf Experience Made a Difference

Our company was doing a mating dance with a Japanese conglomerate. The Japanese decided to visit us at our home office and then see our stores in various parts of the United States to evaluate our company. Prior to their arrival, an agenda was set that included golf as part of their visit. I do not know who was more interested in the golf outing, the Japanese contingent or me. They came with a contingent of four people, the big boss in charge of businesses worth $15 billion, and three underbosses, responsible for $1 billion to $3 billion each. (There was, however, no question of who was the big boss.)

A golf game was arranged at a very nice country club where there were to be two foursomes, the big boss, the underbosses, and myself, with three other local business executives who could certainly benefit from this international relationship. Other than our overseas friends, all were my close friends. My Japanese friends brought no clubs but came with shoes, gloves, and very nice golf apparel, so I arranged to borrow the most up-to-date clubs for my guests. Each had "The Big" driver and graphite-shaft irons. I also brought three dozen logoed balls for the group.

The game started with lunch and then we moved to the driving range before teeing off. The game was going well. The big boss, who belonged to a million-dollar membership fee club in Japan, was clearly the better golfer. The underbosses only played three or four times a year and spent most of their time at driving ranges in Tokyo. But they enjoyed the beautiful scenery and condition of our course; everyone was having a grand time. While there were language problems, the universal hand signals of power and despair were clear to all the players. When language was needed an interpreter shuttled between the foursomes.

On the eighteenth hole, the interpreter came to our carts and seemed very excited. I could not understand anything except the words "Pete Sampras." My Japanese playing companion snatched the scorecard and went bounding across the fairway, yelling to me, "Pete Sampras, Pete Sampras, Pete Sampras." To my surprise, approaching the adjacent ninth hole was Pete Sampras. My Japanese partner waited for Sampras to hit his second shot and then swooped down in his cart for an autograph. I was in shock. But to my great surprise, Sampras signed the scorecard, and then my Japanese partner bounded back across the fairway to the cart. All he kept saying was "Pete Sampras."

We arranged for drinks and hors d'oeuvres in the men's locker room, where we were thanked profusely through the interpreter. The Japanese said it was a day to long remember, but the icing on the cake was seeing Pete and getting his autograph. As a result of this experience, we are currently doing $250 million in business with this conglomerate. When I visit Japan to oversee the joint venture, my Japanese golf buddies always talk about their golfing day in the United States and cannot wait to return for another day.

Think of all of the local agencies, corporations, and independent associations that promote for business. The chambers of commerce in many cities sponsor annual golf tournaments to help their members network for business. Car dealerships, law firms, accounting firms, and virtually every civic club sponsor golf tournaments. Deloitte and Touche, as well as Ernst and Young, sponsor professional golfers who wear their logos. Andersen Consulting annually sponsors a PGA Tour–sanctioned event on fantastic courses. Coopers and Lybrand furnishes the "official" scoreboard at PGA Tour events. Buick, Cadillac, and Prudential are just a few more names that use golf as a promotional tool. Most private clubs have sponsored charity fund-raising events. Entire memberships embrace the event as a way to use their personal networks to the charity's advantage. The tour events couldn't exist without the wonderful volunteers, most of whom are required to pay for the "uniform" worn throughout the tournaments. Banks, insurance companies, and other corporate entities use the tournaments to involve their staffs in charities supported by so many professional events.

What makes golf such a good tool for business development? The answer is simple. Name any other sport or activity where you spend several hours with your playing partner in an intimate, nonthreatening manner, where the atmosphere is fun, calming, beautiful, and where you can develop a solid relationship. Golf is an activity, which if used properly, can help develop better business relationships rather quickly, on a one-on-one basis. In this regard, golf has no peer.

The Score Doesn't Count

To use golf as a relationship and business development tool we need to know how to play the game, manage ourselves around the course, understand the rules and etiquette, and develop good communication skills. A new golfer should take the time and make the investment by taking at least a few lessons from his local PGA professional. The old saying "Practice makes perfect" unfortunately does not apply to golf. No one plays it perfectly. However, weekly practice and a series of lessons could lower your handicap and make the game more fun. Having a golf club, an old wedge or driver, close by in the office just to waggle around, or a putter with one of those funny cups—all of these things help. If we can all enjoy casual Fridays, then we should to be able to grip a club during conference calls on those awful speakerphones. One thing you *can* learn to play perfectly is BusinessLinks, because the score doesn't count!

This does not mean that you should not try to play as well as you can. The objective is to learn how to play with any player, no matter how skilled, without fear or preconceived notions. High-handicap players can learn to play with a tour player with confidence. The key is not the ability to shoot a low score; it's the ability to manage yourself appropriately around the course. A prime example is knowing when to "pick up"—when you pick up your ball if you find yourself shooting for a triple bogey and you still aren't on the green! This simple action helps speed up play and shows consideration for the rest of the group. It also helps relieve pressure if you're having a bad day. The group is still able to play a round at a normal pace and, depending on your course management and communication skills, you can always have a fantastic time.

Conversely, the better player needs to learn how to make the higher-handicap player feel comfortable. He is not there to intimidate the rest of the group. In a BusinessLinks round, or in any round for that matter, the better player should support and encourage the whole group. The host should take the spotlight off himself and put it on the guests, so it does not matter who plays better. We do not encourage the better player to hit bad shots or in any way try to play to the less-skilled player's level. A casual "I'm playing better than I have in years," or "You're bringing me good luck!" can make everyone comfortable. The better player has to learn how to play with the high-handicapper in a manner that eliminates any source of stress. Admittedly, this takes time, but it can be learned.

We all started somewhere and have played our share of poor rounds. For those of us who are highly competitive, again, regardless of handicap, the frustration level certainly can be visible. Therefore, better players should take special care when playing with higher handicappers. Impress them not only with shot-making ability, but more importantly with humility.

Making a Higher Handicapper Feel Good at the World Golf Village

This reminds us of a game played at the recently completed World Golf Village course near St. Augustine. The course, called the Slammer and the Squire, was designed by Bobby Weed with the collaboration of Sam Snead and Gene Sarazen. It served as the site of the ESPN-televised 1998 National Collegiate Athletic Association (NCAA) championships. We played in a threesome due to a last-minute cancellation from a Tallahassee banker. It was the day before the college championships, so the course was in wonderful shape. It is tough, but fair.

The invited guests included a 12-handicap banker from nearby Jacksonville who had not yet played this course, which was right in his own back yard. Rounding out the threesome was a friend from Chattanooga, another low handicapper, whose successful dry-cleaning franchise is expanding into Florida. The owner of the franchise is the consummate business golfer—highly entertaining.

By day's end, we had heard many stories, and each of us had our share of experiences to talk about in this very casual atmosphere. We shared the banking needs for several projects that the banker could fund, and came away from the "meeting" with our homework assignments to get us to the next level with the bank. We agreed on a follow-up game in Chattanooga, where the banker could continue his required due diligence on the franchise owner's company.

When the scores were added in the parking lot, the ecstatic banker had won outright, had shot 79, made three birdies, and had even three-putted the last hole under adverse conditions when the winds were blowing twenty miles per hour. At the first tee, there was clearly a little nervousness on his part, although he may not have admitted it! We had a great time, everyone enjoyed the afternoon, and our business goals were accomplished.

First-Tee Jitters That One Golfer Recalls

About three years ago I had a chance to play with a potential new client at one of the tougher courses in town. I knew that he was a very good player. At the time my game was in need of serious help. We did all the usual things before we got to the first tee, like hit some practice balls. That was a big mistake. I watched this guy hit the ball a mile straight down the fairway. I was a nervous wreck before we got to the first tee. I won the toss but insisted that he go first. Again, he smacked one nearly three hundred yards down the middle. I wanted to crawl back to the cart and say I hurt my back and just watch him the whole day. But the strangest thing happened. He must have sensed I was nervous, because he came up to me and casually said, "That was the best drive I ever hit. Don't worry about yours, I'm going to need your help on the green." His comments really took the pressure off me. I hit a nice shot that went about one hundred yards dead right, and then hit my mulligan about 210 in the short hair. My guest was very humble about his game. Actually, it was wonderful to watch. He repeatedly made it easier for me with encouragement and humor. We ended up having a great day, and we have played several times since. Our relationship is special, and within a short time we were discussing business.

2

Private Versus Public

The Private Club

Many private golf clubs have made it clear that they only want a certain type of member. In order to accomplish a club's objectives, it is not uncommon to find inflated initiation fees (up to $100,000 or more), which essentially limits the membership to a select few. A review committee accepts or denies potential members, regardless of their ability to pay initiation fees. This may not be fair, but it has been this way for years at some clubs. A prospective member has to be referred or sponsored by a member and endorsed by another, and often needs additional letters of recommendation before the application is complete. The intimidation factor in meeting the requirements of personal introductions to various membership committees are still part of the process, and for the most part, help protect a private club's exclusivity. Nevertheless, these clubs are very successful and have long waiting lists.

However, there are many advantages to private golf club membership. Let's spend a little time outlining how to pick the appropriate private club to join. It is not necessary to be a member to be able to learn the game and use BusinessLinks skills. There are more than twice as many municipal and daily-fee golf courses than private clubs. But relationships can be enhanced and business can be conducted just as effectively at public courses between golfers who use their people skills wisely. Here are some of Pat's favorites.

Preston Trail

They serve the best lunch in Dallas. You don't need a starting time; you just walk out and play. They have a rule that you are not supposed to discuss business, but you do.

Winged Foot

You get great treatment from the staff at all of these courses, but it is something special at Winged Foot. The feel of the clubhouse is very warm. With its proximity to New York, you get a feeling that all of the other people at the course are important business-people who are serious golfers. It may look like they are taking time away from business, but they probably are doing more business deals on the course than anywhere else.

About five thousand private clubs exist in the United States; some areas of the country seem saturated with golf. In Broward and Dade counties, Florida, there are over three hundred private and public golf courses, with plans for many more. There are also 8,416 daily-fee, and 2,541 municipal courses, just in the United States. Golf courses are being built at a faster rate than ever before. Developers invariably include some golf activity center in the amenity packages. Designating some of the overall land plan for golf often aids in meeting the environmental requirements that haunt developers. We visualize continued utilization of smaller tracts of land close to heavy employment centers. Pitch-and-putt courses and learning centers will provide nice business opportunities for the entrepreneur who will cater to a busy executive and his or her family.

The Public Courses

Business can be conducted just as effectively at public and private courses between golfers who possess the right communication skills. Public courses can vary from "cow pastures" to wonderful well-maintained operations. There is a host of them, but some favorites include Torrey Pines, in La Jolla, California, site of the Buick Invitational ; Coghill Golf Course, in Chicago, host of the 1997 USGA Amateur Championships; Bethpage Black Course, on Long Island, New York, host of the U.S. Open since the turn of the century; White Columns Golf Course, in Atlanta, Georgia; and World Woods Golf Course, in Brooksville, Florida, voted the best new course in the country. If you run the numbers on the overall cost of entertaining someone on a good public course, you will find that you are much better served on a quality public course than at a "cow pasture." If business is to be done, bite the bullet and go to a good track. No guest, in any business setting, ever became upset over being treated first class.

The Resort Courses

The only other choice you have is to entertain on a resort course. The key here is to find out whether you can play the course as a walk-on, as opposed to being an overnight guest at the resort. You should also check to see whether a tournament is scheduled, and determine whether a major maintenance program is under way or just completed. Every quality resort property has an elaborate tee time scheduling process; they want your business, and they know you will pay the price. The fact is, as long as you are certain that the greens have not been recently aerated or the fairways plugged, the cost of a nice resort round is usually worth it. Essentially, you have our own private club for the day, with no initiation fee, just a slightly higher cost per round. There is no reason why business discussions can't get off the tee as easily here as at a very fine private club. Resort courses are usually special; many are home to professional tournaments, and all golfers enjoy the atmosphere of a tournament site. There is no shortage of fine tracks to host an important business relationship.

TPC Sawgrass, Described by Pat

Although it only opened in 1982, this course is also familiar to your guests because it is the scene of the Players Championship. Certainly, everyone playing the course for the first time can't wait to get to the seventeenth hole, the par 3 with the island green. Whether your shot makes it on or not is something everyone talks about. This is the home course of the PGA tour, and you can be assured that quite a bit of business has gone on there. The practice range is fantastic.

Equity and Nonequity Clubs

Choosing a club usually entails three issues—money, the course, and membership. Assuming that money is not an issue and the course is considered a good track that is well maintained, let's focus on membership. There are two types for private clubs. One is known as an equity membership and the other is nonequity.

Every membership has advantages and disadvantages. The equity membership is similar to buying stock in a company. This type of membership is typically more expensive than nonequity, and both have monthly dues. In an equity membership, the owners of the club are the individuals. Members typically campaign and vote for the board of directors, which manages the club. There are several excellent management companies which handle day-to-day activities, but direction and policy making often rests with the board of directors. Club policy usually dictates when and for what sum the members can sell their memberships. In most clubs, if the membership fee appreciates or depreciates in value, the members can sell their memberships for their current value. Some clubs allow the members to receive a refund of only a portion of their membership fee, regardless of its value. This is usually the case in the very posh and expensive clubs. Many clubs offer no refund, regardless of the cost or length of membership.

Nonequity clubs have an initiation fee plus monthly dues. In this case the members have no voting rights and are bound by the policies and rules set forth by the owner, who may be the developer of the surrounding real estate. Sometimes the developer-owner will have an advisory board, but that is often subject to change at the whim of the owner. It is critical to understand the policies of the club when considering the expense of membership.

Wow! We could have played golf for less than this!

Nonequity clubs are also referred to as semiprivate clubs, because they allow nonmembers to play either at certain times of the year or year-round. This arrangement is typical where there are seasonal differences that affect the amount of play (management wants to ensure a certain amount of cash flow throughout the year). No matter which kind of club you are considering, be sure to understand its policies clearly. Ask questions about privileges, reciprocity with other clubs, tournament committees, limitations on member play, and other conditions that will affect how members enjoy their club.

Meet with the membership director to find out what type of members are on the club's roster. Many clubs have older members who make up the bulk of the membership. If a retirement atmosphere is what you seek, then you've come to the right place. On the other hand, newly developed communities tend to enroll younger, family-oriented members. There has been a marked increase in junior golf programs, which are producing well-rounded future business leaders who learn communication skills at an early age. It makes sense to find and then join a club that meets your entire family's needs. To do so, determine the club's short-term and long-term plans by making the following inquiries:

1. Does the club actively promote new and younger members?

2. What type of membership makes up the club and what are the club's policies, such as accessibility to the golf course for children?

3. Are most members young professionals or retired individuals?

4. Is the club located in the middle of a projected highway expansion?

5. Does the club have regular membership activities to make it easy to meet new people?

6. Does it offer good dining facilities?

7. Is the resident golf professional active in setting up tournaments and pairing new members with other members?

8. Does the course have a good maintenance program?

9. How long has the golf professional and the course superintendent been there?

10. What are their backgrounds?

11. Is the course scheduled for any major reconstruction which would put it out of commission for an extended period of time?

12. Does the club offer a monthly calendar of events or monthly newsletter?

13. Is the club an affiliation club? (There are several large companies that own and manage clubs throughout the United States, and their members have reciprocal rights at affiliate clubs.)

Obviously, there are many details to consider before you join a club. In a private club, it is easier to develop business relationships with members and nonmembers, but not necessarily because the courses are better. Rather, the same groups of friends and acquaintances show up on a regular basis, so you have a better chance of finding a game and getting to know the members. The public courses, some of the world's most challenging tracks, tend to have a more transient field of players, so it takes more time to learn who comes out to play on a regular basis. In any event, people skills can be learned and honed on any golf course, and that is our point.

There are a few private clubs that forbid the use of cellular telephones and beepers not only in the clubhouse, but also on the course. Members go there strictly for the enjoyment of the game, and they don't want to be bothered with business. Generally speaking, the physical facilities are always great. Most of the time the clubs are very expensive, very plush, and very formal. Since each membership is entitled to organize the way it wishes, we should respect that right, and always abide by its rules. Incidentally, if a guest does not go along with the rules at these clubs, chances are he won't be invited again. And if a guest doesn't follow the rules, what are the chances of being able to develop any meaningful relationships?

The Club Staff

To ensure that a club dining experience is going to be a good one, get to know the dining and kitchen staff. If a special effort is made to meet the club's staff, they will appreciate it and your guests will have a much better time at the club. Even at public courses you should introduce yourself and your friends and associates to the resident professional, the general manager, the person behind the counter, or the chef. They all have a part in making the golf experience a good one for you and your guests. The starter and the waiters, and of course the bartender, will contribute to your business guests' golfing experience. Golf industry employees know they are in the hospitality business and want to make your attendance at the club enjoyable. We know a few crabs too, but fortunately those folks are exceptions, and they don't stay around for long. By taking the time to develop a good relationship with the staff (bring them bagels on occasion, or an extra ticket to a sporting event), you will find enthusiastic greetings when they see you—all of a sudden you will feel special! Many clubs insist on the club staff addressing members formally, while other clubs insist on a casual atmosphere. If either is important to you, learn what the club requires.

This Is Doral, One of the Great Clubs

Another course whose reputation excites your guests. They've heard so much about the Blue Monster, a course recently made even tougher by Raymond Floyd's reworking of it. Doral is a great vacation spot, and the facility itself is very nice.

Tips on Tips and Gratuities

Most private courses do not allow tipping, and most members at these clubs abide by the rules. Other clubs include tipping as a routine part of the experience. Some clubs add a 15 percent to 25 percent gratuity on food and beverage bills, while others use a monthly minimum. Some clubs exclude cigars or special functions from the gratuity charges. Christmas gratuities are appropriate to those special employees who are particularly attentive to your needs, but most private clubs have an optional fund that is shared by the entire staff. These gratuities consist of an amount determined by combining a seniority factor and a somewhat subjective manager award. Generally speaking, this method is the least expensive, and because of member volume, it is fairest to all employees. Our recommendation is to follow the rules of the club, and if you wish to do something special for an employee, theater tickets or dinner reservations are appreciated as a token of thanks to those who do an exceptional job making of the golf atmosphere a class act.

An Ohio Banker Makes It Comfortable

Golf can be very awkward, especially if you are not familiar with the club. At your club, you know the rules, the dress code, how to act, if the rangers are going to be helpful in keeping up speed of play; you know the employees and the other members. Of course you know the pro. It's not a cold game, if you will. If I invite a customer to play golf, I set the whole thing up. I make certain before we hit the first tee that he understands the dress code and that this is my course so he will feel comfortable. There are things you do so your guest is never embarrassed. I check to see who is playing in front of us and behind. If he or she turns out to be a slow player, I can go back and tell the folks, "Hey, we're going to be a little slow, let us know when you want to play through." We don't want to be hassled on the course. I make certain that if the pros are around, my guests are introduced. Try to put guests completely at ease. You don't want your guest irritated when you are on the course.

We Deserve It

We know a group of business associates who take an annual trip called the WDI, an acronym for "We deserve it." The outing was the idea of Tampa attorney Bill Chastain. They have visited Pinehurst, Pebble Beach, PGA West at LaQuinta, Reynolds Plantation, Atlanta's Cherokee, Black Diamond, and WorldWoods. There is always too much golf, too many laughs, and sometimes a little too much libation, but it is always a good time. Somebody is in charge of reservations, somebody else chooses all the restaurants, wine is generally a group effort, and somebody else handles the bets, which go into the pot before teeing up for the first round. Partners are chosen ahead of time, and the games are set.

It is a great format, with one round of five usually thrown out for the overall "net" prize, and payoff in cash is immediate following every day's play. A small percentage goes to the "house" for the wine at dinner. Usually the dollars are just swapped around, and if luck is in the air, a golfer might come out a couple of hundred dollars ahead, so nobody gets hurt. It's a terrific way to get together, and everyone looks forward to it. The friendships are valued and, of course, business is conducted between the members of the group. These trips have developed into a social focal point, enhancing personal and business relationships.

3

Communication and Rapport

The eighteenth hole can't come fast enough if the day is going awry!

—Will Rhame

Old Meets New in the Words of Pat Summerall

In the past, golf had a reputation as a staid game, where you couldn't really figure whether you were going to have a good time. Now it's changed to a much more casual atmosphere. People wear shorts instead of long pants. More and more people are playing golf. I see younger golfers, more lady golfers, diversity among the players, and more good golfers. The media exposure is a primary factor, which has helped the quality of the overall golf population. Twenty-five years ago if you were thrown into a group of people there was a higher probability that one of the players would be an unfriendly stuffed shirt, a total hack, or someone who thinks he's above you and wouldn't have time to compete with somebody who couldn't play as well as he did. That's what makes the BusinessLinks program even more important. There are more and more people who have already taken the time to learn how to play the game, so there is no reason someone shouldn't be competent at developing solid relationships.

Examining human behavior in the game has always been a source of laughter, humility, and frustration. Looking at it from a nonprofessional point of view, but one based on experience, we have wit-

23

nessed some of the most ridiculous behavior by golfers of all levels. It's no wonder that thousands and even millions of dollars worth of potential business deals are lost in just one round of golf!

What is it that makes some golfers so unaware of their personal behavior that it is impossible for them to develop any kind of rapport or meaningful relationship with those they invite for a round of golf? An argument could be made that most golfers bring their competitive side to the course. Is this because of their upbringing, or the natural tendency of the survival of the fittest? Is it because of the business environment they live in, where competition to succeed creates such high levels of stress? Whatever the reason, we believe that the intense personal struggle to compete is one of the reasons why so many of us fail at developing relationships during a round of golf. Our focus is on ourselves in order to play well, and some golfers will go to almost any length to achieve that goal.

Humility and honesty is often hard to find on the course. Some golfers let the game's challenges affect their personal behavior in ways that they are not aware. We have found that golfers of all levels have demonstrated poor behavior when the "cranial cramps," "yippers," and other mental blocks challenge our potentially perfect round.

The key to developing relationships is twofold. First, we should develop an understanding about our personal behavior before we try to psychoanalyze others. Second, from that foundation of self-realization, we should learn how to recognize other personalities so that we may adapt or change our behavior in order to more easily develop a bond and hopefully a long-term relationship with our guests.

In practicing a round of BusinessLinks, learning effective communication strategies is one of the easiest elements to understand. It requires grasping a few basic principles of human nature. How we communicate with others will not only help on the course but throughout our personal and professional career.

Listen to Your Guests

We must learn to suspend our personal judgments so that we can listen clearly, and ask appropriate questions in order to determine an individual's needs. Human nature is incredibly strong. Take, for example, the following observation. What is the most used word in any language? We all know the answer: *I.* If that's true, then what does it tell us about our personalities? The most important thing to me is *me,* and the most important thing to you is *you.* Armed with that knowledge, we can learn how to become more effective communicators. The bottom line of a perfect round of BusinessLinks is not about how well you hit the ball, how low your score is, or how far you hit it. It's about your character, honesty, and humor, and how you evoke these qualities to develop a bond with your guest that can last a lifetime. It's learning how to put yourself second and your guest first.

Mickey Mantle's Friendship With Pat

Mickey Mantle and I had the same type of experience through golf. We would play sometimes twice a week. He would begin to ask me questions about what it was like at the Betty Ford Center. He realized that he had a problem, but he didn't want to go in for treatment. As we talked more and more on the golf course, he began to realize his problem with alcohol was serious. He would ask me, "Did you have a good time when you were at the Betty Ford Center?" I told him I wasn't going for a good time. When I said something like that he would stop talking.

The next week the subject would come up again, and he would ask, "What's it like?" Finally, he asked, "Do you think you can get me admitted?" He knew he needed treatment and I knew I could help. I called the Betty Ford Center and arranged to have a bed for him. Unfortunately, his liver illness was too far advanced for him to live much longer, but for the last eighteen months of his life a sober, different kind of personality appeared. When he was drinking he was pretty caustic and crude. The friendship we developed on the golf course led him to feel more and more comfortable discussing something that. was obviously very personal. I'm on the President's Council of the Betty Ford Center and actively help promote the Center for Drug and Alcohol Abuse Rehabilitation, but I had no idea how important golf could be in breaking down the barriers golfers had when talking about sensitive issues.

Effective communication is similar, in that we must learn to suspend our personal agenda so that we can listen clearly to what a person is saying. Communication is a learned activity; we do not come by it naturally.

The same is true with our golf swing. In order to continue to lower our handicap and improve our score, we must learn the basics first, and then practice, practice, practice. Universities are finally teaching more about personal relationship development, while the corporate world has spent countless dollars training employees about more effective communication strategies for sales, business negotiations, and internal productivity. Business golfers can learn volumes to enhance a BusinessLinks round by applying the same principles of effective communication taught by professionals in the academic and corporate arenas.

Pat Summerall Recalls a Seve Story at Augusta

One year at Augusta we were trying to break in a new announcer who knew a lot about auto racing but nothing about golf. He was doing the fourteenth hole as we were rehearsing during a practice round. Then Seve Ballesteros hooked his tee shot into the big gallery on the left. They got to the ball, and Seve and his brother Manuel had their conversation in Spanish. Then, to get the crowd out of the way, they started yelling, "Fore! Fore! Fore!" and the announcer spoke into his mike, "You can hear Seve yelling for his four-iron." Needless to say, our friend never announced a regular round at Augusta.

S. I. Hayakawa Once Said

In our complex and interrelated world, in which the need to understand and to be understood is greater than it has ever been, the cry arises on every hand: How can we communicate better? How can we avoid being misunderstood? How can we get our message across? How can we improve our image? Perhaps the wrong questions are being asked. Perhaps the right questions are: How can we become better listeners? How can we better understand the views of others? The thing to do is to suspend the pursuit of your own goals and listen to the other person—and find out how the world looks to him or her.

How About This Joker

Have you ever played golf with someone who is totally fascinated with himself? He constantly talks about his accomplishments and has little or no interest in you. Let's call him the egocentric golfer. This clown expects praise when he hits a good shot and gets mad when he plays like the rest of the world. He acts as if every shot he makes should be perfect, and the rest of us are mere mortals. This golfer can't stand to lose. He just has no clue of the fundamentals of effective communication. All he knows is the "I" word, and typically has no patience to listen to someone else's story. This is the person who gets invited to play once, but never again. If it was a game of pickup baseball or basketball he'd be picked last, and then only because another body was needed.

Every club has one or two of these members. It's the guy who complains before the ball leaves the club face, the one who thinks it is unfair that the ball is just *barely* out-of-bounds, and only because the cart path should have been in a different place, or the out-of-bounds markers are out-of-line. And then there's his standard complaining about the greens, and the afternoon showers that ruined his day. Oh, yes, he's the same golfer who wants to go out right after a three-inch downpour, with total lack of respect for management's decision to close the course due to the possible damage to it while it is so wet. He is also not required to follow the ninety-degree cart path rule, and he tips the caddie or runner about half of what is normal. He is probably also the guy who goes in to the clubhouse for free coffee and always manages to take a few cookies off the tray, reserved for those who ordered lunch. Sound familiar?

Is it possible that he is also the guy who complains about the Fourth of July event, or a U.S. Open pick-the-pro event? Even if he wasn't so cheap he couldn't get a partner, because he complains about the activities that take his regular tee time. By the way, this is the same guy who spends seven or eight minutes looking for a ball while he holds up the group behind him. Rake a bunker? Forget it. Fix a ball mark? Sure, he'll do that, but he never makes the effort to repair an extra one. Pick up a check? Buy a beer? He sneaks a few in his bag so he doesn't have to support the club! What a pleasure to play a round with this guy. He's the identical fellow who, in a threesome or a fivesome, rides alone! That's good, because we don't really like having to watch him suddenly "find" his ball in deep rough on the other side of the fairway.

While our example may be extreme, there are thousands of golfers whose behavior is aptly described above, and they have no idea of the disturbing effect it has on their playing partners.

We ran across this story, which is just a wonderful example of some of the traits just described. We are told it is true, and someday we'll see it on a sitcom.

Jamie E. Arjona Recalls

Southeastern Idaho is a region with some very intense amateur golf. And it's no wonder, for the golf season there is often quite short, as for lengthy spells it gets downright cold in that part of the country. I once overheard someone call Idaho a state with only three seasons . . . July, August, and winter! For that reason, Idahoans try to get in as much golf as they can, when they can, and many of the courses in the state have lots of tournaments scheduled during the available season, several of them two-day events. It was during just such an event, in the city of Pocatello, Idaho, that the following took place.

Three golf friends and I had entered a four-man, best-ball, two-day tournament played on a city-owned golf course. We were all fairly good golfers and had high hopes of placing well in our division. But many OBs (out-of-bounds) and several lost balls during the first day's round virtually eliminated us from contention. So when we got to the eighteenth tee we all had resigned ourselves to relaxing and just having some fun.

As we arrived at the tee, the foursome ahead of us was preparing to hit away. Included in the foursome was Stanley, a very good golfer. A long knocker, fine iron player, and great putter, Stanley had all of the elements the art of golf demanded. But Stanley also had one very big shortcoming: an explosive temper with a very short fuse.

Stanley was hitting as we arrived. He had a very controlled and purposeful swing with a Fred Couples tempo—a thing of real beauty. He hit a powerful, booming drive straight down the middle of the fairway and held a perfect "Freddie" pose at the finish as he watched the ball in flight. It soared up and out no less than 270 yards, hovering at its apogee for what seemed like an eternity before finally falling to earth. But it did not strike the earth—well, not directly. It landed dead center atop a steel sprinkler head, which caused it to leap high into the air once again, and bounce dead left, off the fairway into some very deep rough.

Stanley could not believe his eyes. With a string of four-letter vulgarities he uncoiled from his perfect finish and proceeded to launch his driver skyward as well. Off it whistled, its sound not unlike that of a helicopter rotor blade. I mean, this club was heading for high altitude. But in its flight it struck the top of a tall spruce tree to the left of the tee. It paused, quivered, and then fell to rest in the highest limbs of the tree. A bald eagle could not have placed it there more perfectly.

Nothing could rival Stanley's wrath now. Screaming every four-letter word he could imagine, he raced around the tee in circles. Finally, he stopped, picked up some sticks and rocks, and began tossing them at his lodged club. But his efforts were to little avail. In fact, one stick which nicked the shaft of the driver seemed to push the club only more deeply into its nest. The other members of Stanley's foursome, thinking better of snickering at his plight, also tried throwing things.

All the activity and noise on the tee caught the attention of a tournament marshal, who quickly drove up to see what was going on. After assessing the situation, he reminded Stanley and his pals of the five-minute rule in effect regarding slow play, and told them that he would have to penalize them two strokes if they did not resume their play immediately. The warning was the last thing Stanley needed at the moment, and he started toward the man with vengeance. Fortunately, a larger teammate tackled him before he reached his target, and with help from others in the group they picked him up, threw him into one of their carts, and headed up the fairway.

I later learned that Stanley, upon reaching his ball in the rough, had simmered down enough to hit a world-class seven-iron from a bad lie in the rough to within a few feet of the pin. He made the birdie putt, and his team led their division by several strokes after the first day of the tournament, which set the tone for what follows.

If a volatile temper and short fuse was Stanley's true handi-cap on a golf course, he had an even more insidious shortcoming when off the course. After a round of golf, Stanley liked to drink. Boy, did he! And that afternoon and evening in Pocatello was no exception. The tournament sponsor always tossed a lavish "end of round one" party. That night Stanley was its star. With what seemed to be a never-empty cocktail glass, and armed with the tale of his travails on eighteen, which he would tell to anyone who would (or wouldn't) listen, Stanley was, it seemed, quite in his element. The more booze he consumed, the more bizarre his tale became. Before long, even the most patient of listeners turned deaf ears to what he said, and he would simply end up mum-bling to himself.

Stanley was one of the last to leave the party that night. It was very dark when he finally poured himself behind the wheel of his car. Fortunately for all, he lived a short distance from the course. Aware of his inebriated state, he drove home slowly and carefully. The thought of his driver still stuck in the tree gnawed at him as he paused in his driveway waiting for his garage door to open. "What to do?" he pondered.

Almost as if by divine providence he heard the answer to his question. When the door fully opened the garage light came on, and there, hanging on the wall, illuminated right in front of him, was his chain saw! "Yes!" Stanley screamed as he leaped out of his car. Grabbing the saw, he jumped behind the wheel, slammed the shift into reverse, and roared back out of his driveway. There was no care nor caution in his driving now, as he put the pedal to the metal and tore back to the golf course. Driving past the club-house, he raced down the road alongside the eighteenth hole and skidded to a stop near the tee. Grabbing his saw, he leaped out of the car, raced up to the tee box, and surveyed the scene. It did not take him long to locate his target. Quickly, he fired up the saw and went to work.

Stanley was not a logger, his chain saw was really quite small, and the tree's trunk was large. So it took him a fair amount of time to drop the big conifer. But finally he succeeded. With a sharp crack the stem of the spruce split and its body toppled over, falling to earth with a loud "whoosh," landing with a final, painful "thump."

"Yes!" Stanley shouted as he danced toward the top of the still quivering tree. "Yes! Yes! Yes!" But he was to never reach his destination. As if on cue, lights seemed to appear from every-where. Red lights, blue lights, white lights, spotlights, flashing lights—they were all around him. And then a very loud voice on a bullhorn declared: "You there, on the tee! This is the police! We have you surrounded! Throw down your weapon—now!"

Stanley was stunned and froze in his tracks.

"This is the police! Throw that weapon down, now! Put your hands on your head, now! Do as I say, now!"

Stanley was arrested and tossed in jail. The charges against him were many, including willful destruction of municipal prop-erty, driving while intoxicated, destruction of the environment, malicious mischief, and even logging without a license. His bail was set at $5,000, which he was unable to post until the follow-ing Tuesday, so in jail he stayed.

Stanley's absence on the second day of the tournament turned his foursome into a threesome. Without his presence they faltered and finished dead last. He had indeed made his mark, quite visibly to each golfer who came up to the eighteenth tee. I even said a few silent words in respect as I passed the fallen spruce, glancing skyward in the quiet hope that my tribute had been acknowledged.

As my thoughts returned to the events at hand, something

So, Stanley, I understand you have a little problem.

caught my attention. I stopped in my tracks and glanced all around. There it was again—a sudden glint of light, reflecting back at me. I moved to my right a bit to get a better view. High atop a tall spruce tree, next to the one Stanley had toppled, light reflected back from something—the shaft of a golf club, Stanley's golf club, his driver, nesting very comfortably where he had left it yesterday. Stanley had cut down the wrong tree!

Stanley went to court for some of the charges against him that night, and was found guilty on all counts. He ended up paying some rather stiff fines and had to perform many hours of community service at—you guessed it—the golf course. As for his driver, a few days later a lineman with the power company happened to spot it. Using the company cherry picker crane, he extracted it and gave it to his son, who had just won a golf scholarship to Arizona State.

Prejudice

Have you ever seen a person for the first time and before you've said a word, you're making assumptions about the person's personality? Maybe it's the clothes worn or the style of hair or the color of skin, or, oh no! It's the opposite sex! Whatever it is, we are constantly judging people before we have any clue as to what really makes them tick. If we all stepped back and looked at ourselves in the mirror, we might be surprised at what we see. Maybe it will help remind us that there is much more to a book than its cover. The human trait of prejudging gets in the way of our ability to communicate effectively. This is very true on the golf course, as we go about sizing up our foursome, the group ahead of us, or those waiting in the fairway behind us.

The next time you play a round of golf, take a different approach. Make an effort to notice how you behave. See if you have a tendency to let the challenges of the game raise your blood pressure or tempt you into taking little liberties that are, quite frankly, against the rules. As a suggestion, play the round without worrying about the score or how well or poorly you hit the ball. You may find yourself playing a different game of golf. If you control your emotions, play exactly by the rules, practice good etiquette, and think about how fortunate you are to be out in such an enchanted atmosphere, then you will begin to understand what a round of BusinessLinks is all about. For some this may take a little practice, and will certainly take some patience. It seems that every club has a few golfers who play consistently well, almost blindly play to their handicap, and always come out ahead at the end of the competition. They know how to play competitively but still be relaxed and engaging in their group, and these players are never short in finding a game.

Pat Summerall Remembers Mac Davis

Most people know Mac for his singing, but he also wrote many of Elvis Presley's big hits, like "Blue Suede Shoes." He's a very good player, a 4-handicapper without looking like one. He's one of those guys who you think is going to shoot 85, but then you look at the scorecard and he's in the seventies and having a ball. He never gets in trouble and hits everything with a slight right-to-left draw.

In a round of BusinessLinks you may not talk about business until the "nineteenth hole," the next game, six months, or a year down the road. The idea is to know when to see the opening, and when to ask the right questions. You have at least four hours in front of you on the first tee, so focus your attention on the needs of your guest. Get into the game and be a great host. Make the golf game experience something you and your guests remember. Establish the relationships, enjoy the whole scene, and get comfortable. The business, if it is meant to be, will literally fall into your lap (assuming you follow up).

Focus Attention on Your Guests, Not on Your Score

(BusinessLinks First Commandment)

Golf has a tendency to unveil our true personalities, and all the little idiosyncrasies we each possess. It can be a very humbling game. The course can bring you to your knees, and how you react to it can affect the potential relationships you are trying to develop. It's not hard to determine a golfer's personality while on the course. The serene and sleepy grasses, tranquil ponds, mystical trees, and perfectly manicured bunkers can suddenly turn into a challenging tempest of golf ball-eating creatures that test the patience of every level of golfer.

4

Dealing With Different Personalities

Golf is the only sport where personalities, and all our idiosyncrasies, show their ugly little heads, so to speak. The key is to assess your guest's personality to determine the best communication strategy in order to develop that all-important rapport. Let's describe two types of personalities. (Don't worry, there is no quiz at the end, but this may remind you of one of the college courses you took.)

Dominant-Aggressive

A dominant or aggressive personality will typically play golf under his terms and will set the tone as to the type of communications that he will allow. He may be there to play golf strictly for sport, or to focus on setting his best score ever. Frustration will come easily to him, and praise will be expected after a good performance. Some of those awful personality traits we described earlier may also be part of the routine, and this person, incidentally, may be a terrific golfer.

How do you deal with a strong personality who is highly competitive and the most important thing to him is the score? Help him achieve his goal. Such people usually have huge egos. Feed them. Leave your own in your bag! Congratulate the good shots. If a bad shot happens, and it will, give encouragement for the next shot. Offer advice on how far it is to the pin, or to the hazard. Make use of the "gimmie."

If he is a better player than you, be sure to "pick up" your ball if you are looking at a triple bogey and are still not on the green. Keep up the pace, and don't slow the group down. Be relaxed and show humor, after all, it's just a game!

We recommend that you always play in a team format in a round of BusinessLinks. This helps take the pressure off you and your guest, because the focus is on the team, not the individual (more on that in chapter 12).

If you are the better player, be careful not to alienate or frustrate your playing partner because of your skill and his natural tendency to want to win. Keep the spotlight on your guest, not on yourself. If he is having a poor day, try to get his mind off the game. Learn a few good short jokes. When you're at a point where you have to wait, or the turn from the ninth hole to the tenth, let loose and tell one. Keep the atmosphere light and you will have a better chance of developing the relationship in a positive way.

Golf has been described as "good cursing practice." Earthy jokes are generally not for BusinessLinks relationships. We have to admit that there are some hilarious jokes centered around the game, but be careful about jokes that couldn't be told anywhere; it doesn't really impress, other than negatively, and it's impossible to make a good second impression.

A Great Example of a Grand Faux Pas

I played in a pro-am a few years ago with a woman tour player as the fifth person in our group. The rest of us had played a million rounds together, so we knew each other quite well. A joke or two was told, and admittedly they were a little crude. On the next tee, the professional pulled us off to the side and told the raunchiest joke, then another three or four. Believe it or not, we were all shocked. Each time I see this professional golfer on television, I don't recall any of the jokes, but I do recall that I don't care to play with her again. Incidentally, she has done quite well on the professional tour. Maybe the jokes work well in other pro-ams, but it didn't do much for our group's first and lasting impression of the golfer.

Don't Push It

Be cautious in assessing a guest's needs on the course. Some dominant personalities take offense if you try to discuss business while playing. We don't recommend discussing business during a round of BusinessLinks if it becomes distracting when trying to focus on the game itself. Assume that most people play golf to have fun and to get away from the office. On the other hand, if your guest starts talking about business, then by all means comply. However, unless you are truly skilled at BusinessLinks, we recommend that you discuss business in moderation on the course. You will have plenty of time at the nineteenth hole or at a later time to continue the discussion or close a deal.

At a cocktail party, when you see a dominating person controlling a conversation with a passive one, who usually wants to leave? The passive person is waiting for someone else to join them so he can move on. Well, in golf, it's not that easy. Not only can the game itself and the course be intimidating, imagine that the person you are sitting next to is your opposite personality type, and he is potentially critical to your future business success. You *have to* figure out a way to get through this day, especially if you are playing poorly. In this case you certainly need to know the rules and etiquette of the game if you are going to survive the round and hopefully succeed with your goals.

Think about it. You are with one or three individuals for several hours. They will all get a pretty good idea of the type of person they are playing with: Can he be trusted? Is he fair? Does he cheat? Is he too loud? Does he get mad? Does he give up if he is not playing well? Is he obnoxious? Does he talk too much? Does he play by the rules? Is this a person with whom I want to do business? If he tells a dirty joke now, would he do the same thing in a business setting?

Subordinate-Passive

A subordinate or passive individual may be a person of few words or one who is constantly asking for help or direction (such as how far is it to the green or what club he should use). He will typically play under whatever terms you recommend and take things personally if he plays poorly.

How do you communicate on the course with a passive personality? Sometimes it's difficult to determine what he is thinking. Responses to your questions may be close-ended. So use a little common sense and ask open-ended questions to get him to relax. Show him the great time you are having. Talk about the course history or where the target is down the fairway. When you hit a bad shot, be jovial about it, and just keep the game lively.

If you are the better player, recognize that your game could be intimidating. Remove the pressure by discussing things other than golf. At this point it doesn't matter who is the host and who is the guest. Provide encouragement by pointing out the good parts of his game, and always be very humble about your own.

If he is a better player than you, the same rules apply from the example above. In a round of BusinessLinks, the group has committed to several hours together. That's a lot of time. There's no rush. Relax. Have a cool drink. Offer the others in the group a good cigar. (Notice the word *good*. There is nothing more disturbing than to be offered one of those terrible, stale, dried-out cigars.)

Again, your goal is to develop rapport and a strong personal bond, and that only happens when ego is suspended and attention is focused on the guest.

How Do Sports Psychologists Assess Differences in Personalities?

According to Richard Jensen, a sports psychologist, and Roy Spungin, a psychotherapist, a person's course demeanor is a clue to their office behavior. Here is what we found out. See where your personality fits.

Director   On the course, the director takes charge, controls the pairings and the type of game to be played, plays to win, and is product-oriented rather than people-oriented. In the office, the director is obsessive-compulsive, makes quick decisions, and can exhibit a dictatorial style.

Participator   Plays for fun, acknowledges members of a foursome as individuals, suggests pairings based on similarities, a consen-

It has come to my attention that one of you lost
to one of our clients in a round of golf!

sus-builder in the office, the participator seeks opinions before making decisions and gains trust from others.

Organizer Enjoys taking risks, betting on the game, steely cool when a loser, grand when a victor, charming and charismatic in the office, attains business goals through thrill-seeking, likes fast-action jobs.

Coach While playing golf, assists others to take focus off self, classic good sport, somewhat insecure. Congenial in the office, the coach is supportive and an excellent manager in a secure environment.

Pat Summerall is no psychologist, but he had the following comments about some famous personalities.

Bill Parcells's Playing Routine With Pat Summerall

Playing with Bill is an experience. He has a little saying, a New Jersey saying, for every kind of shot. Every shot has an identifying name. I could write a book about all those crazy names! He's a lot of fun to play with.

Deane Beman Focuses On the Task at Hand

Unquestionably, the best business golfer I've ever been around was Deane Beman. As intense as he was about playing, he was more intense about the business of golf. He made more deals on the golf course than anybody. That was one of the keys to his success as the commissioner of the PGA Tour.

He never lost sight of his business objective, no matter how entwined his thoughts might be with how he was playing. He was a master at weaving golf in with what he was trying to accomplish from a business standpoint. You were always aware that he had some thoughts about how the game fit into his business plan. The fact that he could do the two things at the same time was one of his great attributes. It was fun playing with him, but you knew there was another motive.

He showed a lot of concern about the game itself. He was very meticulous about the rules. You don't touch the ball, you don't improve lies, and there was no such thing as a mulligan. He knew the rules.

He usually got the job done, and if he didn't, he would get a rematch.

Ken Venturi—No Patience, but Plenty of Fun

I've played with Ken countless times. He has absolutely no patience. If he has to wait he can't stand it. He has to go where the action is. If you play with him, you might play the fifth hole first, then seventeen, then twelve.

Chuck Daly—Loves the Magic of Golf

The former coach of the Detroit Pistons and current head coach of the Orlando Magic just has a good time on the course. He loves to tell jokes. He's still serious about playing, but making the relationship work and having a good time comes first.

No matter who you invite for a round of BusinessLinks, you must establish a high level of rapport if you expect to be successful in realizing your business goals. Establishing rapport is ι and most effective way to develop a solid relationshι has to do with being somewhat like, or appealing to the iι another person. You establish it by subtlely emphasizing .ιays in which you are similar and playing down the ways you are different, with the hope of addressing your business somewhere along the line, perhaps at the end of the day. You don't have to like someone to have rapport with him, but you do have to act like him in some ways, or at least develop a basis of mutual interest.

Do We Really Play Golf Naked?

We couldn't resist sharing the following excerpt from a wonderful book by Michael Murphy called *Golf in the Kingdom* which illustrates the point. The scene is Scotland, a typical round at Burningbush has just ended, and we're at the dinner table.

Picture This Scene

"Awright, I'll tell ye what I think, for through my sufferin's a certain understandin' has developed." He looked with sad eyes around the table and winked at Julian. "If I've learned one thing about the game, it is that 'tis many things to many people, includin' the many ones in my very own head." He tapped his temple. "We've certainly seen them come and go through Burnin' bush. Tall ones, short ones, scratch players, and duffers from the end o' the warld. Intellectual sorts and workin' men, pleasant temperaments and mean ones, the MacGillicudys and the Balfours, the Leviases, the St. Clairs, the Van Blocks, the gentlemen from Pakistan—in terms of origin and character and ideas, a most diverse and complex lot. For each has his peculiar understandin', his peculiar theory, his peculiar view o' the world, his peculiar swing, God knows. Get them here on the links, and all their parts fall oot." He smiled sadly again and shook his head "Gowf is a way o' makin' a man naked. I would say tha' nowhere does a man go so naked as he does before a discernin' eye dressed for gowf. Ye talk about yer body language, Julian, yer

style o' projectin', yer rationalizashin', yer excuses, lies, cheatin' roonds, incredible stories, failures of character—why, there's no other place to match it. Ye take auld Judge Hobbes, my God, the lies he told last week about that round o' his in the tournament, 'tis enough to make ye wonder about our courts o' law. So I ask ye first, why does gowf bring out so much in a man, so many sides o' his personality? Why is the game such an X-ray o' the soul?"

Is Golf Like a Marriage?

For those of us who are or have been married, the single biggest challenge is interpersonal communications. We have to work hard at it. Ideological perceptions, social status, and tradition have a tremendous effect on our ability to communicate. How can you possibly know how I feel if you can't hear me? Listening carefully includes being able to understand what the other person is saying. Do you listen closely to what the person says, or are you already thinking of a response?

In the case of golf, think about how easily most of us interact with one another in a positive, nonthreatening, fun way. We make the effort to communicate effectively by listening at least on a social level. The golf course is where men sometimes act like boys and women sometimes communicate as they would at the hairdressers. We let our hair down. We go to extraordinary lengths to have a good time. For those of us in significant relationships, if we would spend the same quality time—four hours—with that person, once a week, as we do on the golf course with our friends or business relationships, we might lower the divorce rate by 70 percent!

More From Burningbush

"Now let's take this thing ye call projection," he looked again at Dr. Laing. "One man sees the Burnin' bush Links as a beautiful thing, the next sees it a menacin' monster. Or one man'll see it friendly one day and unfriendly the next. Or the same hole will change before his very eyes, within minutes. . . . On some days I love these links of ours, on others I hate them. And it looks different, by God; it looks different dependin' on my mood. Agatha

here says I go through the same kind o' trouble with her, guid woman." He reached toward his wife. "Like marriage it is, like marriage!"

The idea seemed to have struck him for the first time. He and Agatha looked at each other in silence for a moment. The sounds of silverware striking plates and slurping of broth quieted as the two of them exchanged secret knowings. All heads turned up from the dinner and looked to the end of the table. Peter and Agatha were sharing untold numbers of insights and feelings regarding the relationship of golf and marriage, and the group seemed to be awed by the sight. Six faces waited expectantly in the candlelight.

"Just like marriage," Peter said at last, in a quiet, solemn voice. Then he turned toward us with a small boy's smile of discovery. . . . turning back to look at her with his child-like smile. "Marriage is a test of my devotion and my memory that things will be all right."

Words of approval and congratulations sprang from all sides of the table. We all wanted to cheer them on. I could see that Agatha was his mother and younger lover and God knows what other incarnations . . . "A good marriage is as rare and complex and fragile as the world itself . . . and very like the game o' gowf . . ."

Then our host and devoted husband broke into an impassioned speech comparing marriage to golf. The connection had sprung some trapdoor of insight and lyricism in his heart, and all his sufferings and enthusiasms poured forth. Like golf, marriage required many skills, he said, "Steadiness of purpose and imagination, a persistent will and willingness to change, long shots and delicate strokes, strength and deft touch," the metaphors were tumbling in all directions now, "good sense and occasional gamble, steady nerves and a certain wild streak. And ye've got to have it all goin' or the whole thing goes kaflooey." He clenched his fist and turned his thumb down. "Any part o' the game can ruin the whole. Ye've got to have all yer parts and all yer skills, yer lovin' heart, yer manhood, and all yer subtleties.

*Not only are ye naked to yourself and to yer partner, but ye've got
to contend with yer naked self, all yoor many selves."*

No matter who you invite for a round of BusinessLinks you must
establish a high level of rapport if you expect to be successful in
establishing your business goals. Establishing rapport is the
quickest and most effective way to develop a solid relationship.
Rapport has to do with being somewhat like the other person or
appealing to their interests. You establish it by subtlety, emphasizing the ways in which you are similar and playing down the
ways you are different, with the hope of addressing your business somewhere along the line, perhaps at the end of the day.
You don't have to like someone to establish a rapport with him
but you do have to act like him in some ways, or at least develop
a basis of mutual interest.

Leave Your Ego in Your Bag

(BusinessLinks Second Commandment)

There are a million ways to open conversations, and volumes
have been written on the subject. We are on a golf course, stuck
together for several hours, and we simply want to understand
each other better. Here are a couple of techniques, one verbal and
one nonverbal, which have proved to keep the ice thawed. These
all work well, and they are simple.

Mirror movements   Following the movements of another person
is called crossover mirroring. This is when one person crosses
his legs and then the other person does the same. Example: Your
guest is on the fourth tee and you notice that he likes to wash
his ball before teeing off, so you do the same. Or you notice he
likes to talk about sports or family—so you do the same. Maybe
he puts his feet up on the rail of the cart, which is nothing more
than a sign of being relaxed. Do something similar that gets across
that you too are relaxed, but be subtle. Don't go overboard, just
try to create a relaxed atmosphere in which you can have an open
discussion with your guest.

Ask questions about your guest   Appeal to his sensitivity. Inquire about family, kids in college, if the spouse plays golf, sports, what he thinks of the course, the name of his favorite course, when he took up the game, or any questions which evoke an interest in developing a relaxed scenario for the day.

Never Again

We are reminded of a gentleman who participated as a guest in his first invitation to Tampa's Gasparilla Invitational, a premier fifty-year-old amateur event played on a fine old Donald Ross 6,200-yard tough track. Year in and year out the tournament attracts some of the country's finest amateur golfers, and it has been won by several tour players just before they turned professional. Prior winners include folks like tournament record-holder Bob Murphy, and PGA champion Hal Sutton. The field always includes current or past winners of the U.S. Amateur, like Fred Ridley or, years ago, Nathaniel Crosby. Two-time British Amateur champion Dick Siderof makes an annual appearance, as does U.S. Amateur runner-up Buddy Marucci. Many times Walker Cup, Mid-Amateur, Senior Amateur, and Porter Cup players tee it up with the rest of the lucky field of competitive golfers.

This guest had a very low handicap, was stuck on himself, and was unwilling to enjoy the round because he was having a bad day. His playing partners had a combined handicap of maybe 8 or 9, so it's not like he was in a group against whom he couldn't compete.

Honor on the tee was not handled correctly, and after he hit his drive he would simply start down the hole, off in the rough, before the rest of the group teed off! At the turn stand he was rude, jumping in front of spectator members who were at the club to watch this fine tournament. He just refused to engage in any meaningful conversation with the rest of the group, none of whom were playing to their handicaps. He had his own caddie, so he sulked in his own little world. The difference was that the rest of the foursome was thoroughly enjoying the day, thankful to be invited to a first-class tournament and grateful for the camaraderie experienced each year at this event, which somehow included this stubborn, selfish jerk.

The faux pas happened time and time again until, finally, it was really having an effect on the ability of the rest of the low handicappers to perform as well as they could. We suspect this guest probably will need to keep his day job, and it may have been his last invitation to that event. Funny thing, he probably is not even aware of his bad manners that day, and he was noticeably absent from the awards ceremony. The point here, of course, is to recognize our own shortcomings and deal with them in a way that does not take away from the group's fun, whether it is a premier amateur event or just another "walk in the park," as we sometimes refer to our weekly rounds of golf.

Even though technology is making it more difficult to recognize a person's true personality (because we do so much business over the phone, fax, and Internet), we still want to feel comfortable about the person with whom we do business. If we are more comfortable with that individual, we stand a better chance of consummating a deal. Common sense tells us that it takes a genuine effort and plan of attack to create rapport in any setting. The golf course is the most powerful arena in the world to develop rapport and long-term relationships. A good experience makes following up in the office setting, over the phone, or the Internet effortless. Depending on how you conduct yourself on the golf course and how you develop the skills needed to bond with fellow golfers, the follow-up after the game can be amazingly easy or incredibly futile.

Understanding human behavior and practicing these basic fundamentals of communication are effective in *all* areas of your life, both on and off the course.

5

Women in Golf

The fastest growing segment of the golf world is women. This has had a very positive impact on the game. The Ladies Professional Golf Association (LPGA) has a tremendous following and is growing rapidly. The Executive Women's Golf Association, started in 1991, now boasts more than fourteen thousand members in eighty-three chapters nationwide, adding chapters every month. In Atlanta there are waiting lists for entry into the women's leagues. Tournament competition is creating excitement across the country, with scrambles and four-balls as well as individual play. No doubt, new relationships are developing, and new business is being done, too. More importantly, golf has opened up in a big way to an appreciating segment of the game, and clubs all over the world are now enjoying the benefits of having a larger audience to use their facilities.

Some of the top executives in the world are women. More women are rising to high-level management positions, and they are recognizing the value of building strong personal relationships through golf. Women seem to have an extra sense, and they are more intuitive than men regarding subjective thinking. While some men are apt to rely on logic, women use both logic and emotion. The point is that women recognize the benefits and power of BusinessLinks. Men need to understand and recognize that, more and more, BusinessLinks is going to be coed. There will be more moms with daughters and sons on the golf course, there will be more couples playing together, and soon there will be more women in the one-day member-guest tournaments. The charity golf scene has already seen a new source to fill the fields, and it is no longer unusual to see many charity fields with a strong representation on the course by women. Business opportunities are no longer restricted to male golfers.

A Story From an Executive Woman Golfer

A vendor had invited me to play golf with him one Wednesday afternoon. We had lunch in the clubhouse, as is typical. While preparing to play, I noticed that there were no other women around the clubhouse dressed in golf attire. We were paired with a grandfather playing with his grandson and were enjoying the round. After about five holes, the club manager drove out and asked to speak with my vendor privately. He reminded him that Wednesday afternoon was restricted to men only.

A Prominent Woman Golfer Says

I highly recommend businesswomen's involvement in the sport. I encourage them to take golf lessons, especially if they have strong ambitions to succeed in business or sales. Women who play golf will have a definite edge in their career and business paths. Every time they tee up they have a four-hour advantage on the competition, and just as much additional exposure to their customers and coworkers.

A Woman Bank Executive Told Us

Huge growth is expected in golf as a business development tool, and it won't just be taking male clients to play, as women are playing in increasing numbers and many of them are prospective clients.

The bottom line is exactly the same for women as it is for men regarding BusinessLinks. You must learn how to manage yourself effectively on the course and focus on building a personal relationship instead of trying to shoot a good score. Who knows, the next round of BusinessLinks you play may be with the opposite sex.

I have made up my mind and there is nothing you can
say, Harris. I hope my firing you won't affect our
marriage in any way.

The Woman Executive Continues

*After being awarded the business, I had been involved in a rather
lengthy and arduous closing process, and we had reached a
standstill in the negotiations with the attorneys. Friday rolled
around and we still had not agreed to the details. I suggested a
face-to-face meeting. My prospective client responded that he
liked to play golf on Friday afternoons and mentioned a particular club where he had been dying to play. As it turned out, my
attorney happened to be a member there and arranged for the
four of us to play that afternoon. We hammered out the details in
a less threatening environment and closed the deal!*

Mulligan

- Golf is a $15-billion-dollar annual business, and growing.
- Ninety-eight percent of Fortune 500 CEOs pick golf as their
  sport of choice.

- The average golfer spends $600 per year on golf.

- Golf is played in a nonthreatening atmosphere, where personal and business relationships can flourish.

- The fastest growing segment in golf is women.

- In BusinessLinks, the score doesn't count.

- It doesn't take more than a little common sense to make a higher handicapper feel comfortable.

- You can effectively develop business relationships on private, public, or resort courses.

- Check the membership list and talk to the director before joining a private club.

- Ask all the questions you need to raise regarding your personal and business needs so that you are certain this club will fit all your needs.

- Develop a relationship with *all* the staff.

- Suspend your personal agenda in order to listen clearly.

- Don't prejudge your guests; give them a chance. Wouldn't you want the same?

- Put your guests first and yourself last.

- Take the time to understand and learn how to communicate with different personalities.

- Rapport develops slowly; don't push it.

- Keep the conversation and jokes clean.

- Relax, play with humility, and don't be afraid to "pick up" your ball.

- Always remember your ultimate goal in a round of BusinessLinks: developing friendships!

Part II

PLANNING THE OUTING

6

Setting Goals

Knowing who is the ultimate decision-maker, or how to get to the UDM, is one of the things that takes time in planning an outing. We should recognize that BusinessLinks is another form of marketing, which requires a little more thought than many successful marketing techniques. In any other business situation where we spend the time and money to market our products or services, there is normally a plan that includes all aspects of the ultimate goals. BusinessLinks is no different. Careful consideration needs to be made regarding who it is you are going to invest the time and money in. Is this person the UDM, or can this individual reach the ultimate decision-maker?

Clifford Roberts, and the Initial Interview with Pat Summerall

My first year at Augusta, I remember my initial meeting with Clifford Roberts, who was then the guru at Augusta National, the chairman of the tournament upon whose word everything revolved.

I had been in broadcasting long enough to know that I wanted to report on golf. For some reason the powers that be at CBS were reluctant to put someone into the tower who wasn't a golfer. They finally picked me to be the eighteenth hole commentator, and I went to Augusta. One of the things you had to do was have an audience with Clifford Roberts.

The executives were deathly afraid of losing the contract at Augusta, and still are. So they arranged for me to meet Mr. Roberts in his apartment in the main clubhouse. Now there were long pauses in anything that Mr. Roberts said. He would say something and the silence would last for what seemed like an eternity.

I came in and introduced myself, and there were just the two of us. He said, "Son, you know, more people know you from football than from golf."

I said, "Yes, sir, I'm aware of that."

Long pause, then he said, "What's your handicap?"

I said, "About twelve."

Another longer period of silence, and then he said, "Well, the best announcer we've ever had here at Augusta was Chris Schenkel, and he was an eighteen, so you'll be okay." And with that he dismissed me. That was my audience.

Planning Can Take More Time Than the Round

All too often we assume that the person we invite for a round of golf is the right one, and only after we are on the course or in the nineteenth hole do we find out we were wrong. Planning in BusinessLinks may literally take more time than the round itself. It's important to find out as much about the person you are going to play golf with and why golf may help the relationship. What is the goal, and is there more than one? Are you prepared? How can you make this round of golf turn into an experience your guest will always favorably remember, an experience that may give you an extra edge when it is time for the business decision?

If you have determined that your guest *is* the right person to facilitate your ultimate goals, then you need to determine where to stage the game. As we discussed earlier, generally speaking, the better the course, the better the experience. If you are a member of a private club, your course may be the right venue. But, as suggested earlier, it is a good idea to come up with another resort or public course if your own club is undergoing a major maintenance program or if a tournament is being played.

From an Accountant Trying to Say Thanks to a Client

I had been introduced to an executive of a major bank who was responsible for awarding the contracts to build bank branches. To fill out the foursome, I wanted to ask a general contractor client whose company could build whatever construction might be awarded. The contractor client had been very loyal to my firm over the years, and this was a way to say thank you. The fourth person was one of the bank's commercial loan officers, responsible for referring several clients in the past. All the golfers had less than 10 handicaps. My home club was in wonderful condition, and I was looking forward to a productive afternoon, saying thanks to a couple of folks who had been good to our firm while networking a potential new relationship to my contractor client.

The contractor shocked me when I called for the invitation. He told me that he didn't really like my home course, a classic Donald Ross design, because it was just too tight, with too much left out of bounds (on thirteen holes), and his game (remember, he had a low handicap) was right-to-left. He appreciated the invitation—but perhaps another time. I hung up, thought to myself, and called another contractor client (who had a 22 handicap). We had a great afternoon, and the contacts blossomed for the client. He developed the relationship and built several bank branches, along with a major renovation of the bank's headquarters.

I eventually quit doing business with the first contractor, and he never knew the real cost of that selfish turndown.

By the way, if caught in a potentially uncomfortable situation at the invitation stage, the rest of the event will likely go downhill. It is best to gracefully get across to the other party that some other time may be better. Always be cordial. In a later chapter we will discuss this point in more detail.

Finally, give your potential guest two or more options as to when you can play. Then the decision to play can be made right away, and your planning can continue. This assumes, of course, that you are planning a casual round, not a scheduled tournament. This is one area where most salespeople need work. Often salespeople use golf more as a recreation or escape from work, not as a business development tool, inviting their friends rather than potential prospects or clients. Additionally, there is typically no method of tracking the results of the outing. Management has no way of determining the success of its sales staff when entertaining prospects and clients on the golf course.

We heard one story from a New Orleans friend who described the two partners of an accounting firm who were relatively new members of the club. They joined it ostensibly for business reasons, yet were always found playing golf with other members of the firm or with each other. He thought it strange that there was never a client or prospect involved in the games the two partners arranged, an unusual business practice. There may have been several reasons for this. First of all, the firm more than likely paid the cost of membership, even though it is not deductible. The two members were the decision-makers, so who would question the expenditure? But the other side of the coin said that they were thoroughly enjoying the club, and so what if they didn't entertain! If they were having fun, who cares? At some point, it may have been strictly a personal expenditure. It is easy to question someone else's motive for joining a club, but we ought to keep that to ourselves and just enjoy the golf.

We suggested to our friend that he ask one of the partners to join his group when it was appropriate. A few weeks later we heard that the two quickly had developed a friendship, and he was actually talking about changing accounting firms. They had already enjoyed several social occasions following their first game. Sometimes including a new member can create goodwill and opportunity that can't be anticipated or measured.

Incidentally, a very effective way to nurture a new business relationship is to combine the business prospect with a good friend or two to complete the foursome. Where a soft, subtle, slow sell is anticipated, friends can add much to the congeniality of the group and actually help the bonding process. We have one friend who kids around when he is asked to join his CPA in a business golf game, and it has happened countless times over the years when a fourth person is needed to complete the group. Usually, within the first two holes he reminds the new prospect that he will get his short form done for about $1,500, and he is sure that his CPA is very fair with his fees—that breaks the ice in a casual, funny way, and always gets a laugh.

7

Playing With Club Professionals

Most players don't realize that the club professional, as well as the assistants, are often available to play. The pro can help make the overall experience a wonderful memory for guests. If you only have one or two guests, try asking your pro if he will play along with your group. This should be arranged in advance, and you should be certain to know the protocol with respect to offering the professional a gratuity. If it is a membership club, learn the custom of the place from one of the board members, or even the general manager. If it is a public course, there is most likely a general manager who can offer some guidance. A gratuity may be in order for the time spent with you and your guests, as long as that is normal for the club. He may or may not take it, but know what is appropriate. To make the point from the professional's side, it is the socializing with members and their guests that often results in the golf shop inventory being reduced in subsequent days and weeks.

Many golf professionals do not mind at all being asked to play. Let's face it, if they *don't* want to play, they will likely give you a polite, "Sorry, I can't schedule it for today," or some other gesture that tells you it just is not in the cards this particular day. Perhaps one of the assistant professionals can join the game. On the other hand, the golf professional is in business too, so there could be a very appreciative yes on the other end of your invitation. If the pro accepts, you will often find a willing helper to add to the foursome, but don't expect it, and certainly don't expect to get a private lesson while out on the course! Some members may think that it's the golf professional's job to be available to the golfers at almost any time. While that is not necessarily the case, more than likely your group can be accommodated, as long as it is done within a schedule, and the golf professional's time is not taken advantage of. The next time you bring a guest, see how the red carpet comes out if you have established a good relationship with the golf staff.

One of Our Golf Friends Remembers the Bogey Pro

This brings to mind a club professional in Orlando who was fondly called the Bogey Pro. Pat Neal was always willing to play with the members. He was a wonderful instructor to adults and juniors alike, and yet it was not uncommon for him to shoot a 75 or 80. But he had such class, was always friendly and accommodating to the membership, and on his day off, which was Monday or Tuesday, he could be found playing golf with a group of members at his own club. Do we see that in football or baseball? What a wonderful role model Pat was to the entire club, including many junior golfers who went on to careers in golf.

Some companies use golf as a personality test before they hire a new employee. These companies invite their potential employee for a round of golf with the objective of observing how this person handles stress. They also find it easier to communicate with the individual and find out more about their personality, family life, likes, and dislikes. By witnessing firsthand how this individual conducts himself on the course, they can judge character, humor, and honesty. Many employers believe they can find out more about a person through a round of golf than in an interview across the desk.

Carefully Choose All the Members of Your Group

(BusinessLinks Third Commandment)

This Guest Has Been Practicing Surgery, Not Golf

I learned a big lesson several years ago during a member-guest tournament at my club. I was trying to get in with a doctor's clinic for insurance purposes, so I invited one of the doctors to play as my guest in the tournament. He said that he had about a 16 to 18 handicap but hadn't played for quite some time. We were teamed up with two other players we didn't know. The good doctor went up to the first tee and completely missed the ball on his first swing. I wish I could tell you it got better, but it didn't. The pressure to win was on, of course, and he couldn't hit a ball to save his life. I thought that he would help us to some extent on the green, but no way. I really felt sorry for the guy. He was trying so hard and getting so frustrated I thought he was going to cry. He couldn't get off that golf course fast enough. He felt humiliated, and in a situation like that there was really nothing I could do. A few days later, when I tried to make an appointment to sell the medical group some insurance, I couldn't get the guy to call me back. I'll never do that again.

Round Out the Foursome

If you are entertaining just one guest, consider inviting one or two other players who could help you with the relationship you are trying to establish. If the game is planned, you'll easily find another friend in the same "twosome situation," and they may gladly join your group. This is a very important element in planning your round. For example, if you are a stockbroker or insurance broker and you invite a potential client for a round of BusinessLinks, do some research on your prospect's background. If he owns a manufacturing company, you may want to invite a supplier for certain components he may use. You may have found out that he is trying to expand his business, so invite a CPA or banker as well. You may have found out that he is from England, so if you know someone from England, invite your British friend to enhance the experience. You enhance the game in many ways through the type of people you invite. You can easily make the experience even more enjoyable with a little extra planning.

Confirmation Note

After you have agreed to a particular day and time, assuming it is a few days away, a confirmation note adds another very professional touch. This gesture is rarely done, but the impact is fantastic. The note can be as informal as a handwritten reminder, or a specialty card that gives the directions, arrival time, tee time, course rating and length, dress code, and a personal note from you. Remember, this is business. Just because you are having the time of your life doesn't mean you should not approach the outing with a good marketing plan.

Different formats provide for different opportunities. The key is simple. Do a little research, find out what your guest likes, his handicap, the last time he played, and if there are complementary business associates that may lend leverage to the outing, and then orchestrate it to benefit all parties.

The essence of BusinessLinks is to do, within reason, everything you can to make your guest's golf experience the most enjoyable possible. You are the ambassador for that particular course on that particular day. You are a caddy, the "host with the most," the waiter, golfer, and butler.

8

Tee Times

Obtaining tee times early in the morning and on weekends can be a challenge. Many public courses now have the starting times set up through an electronic answering service. In those situations, knowing somebody at the golf shop doesn't work anymore. Your best chance to play at your preferred time is to be the first caller. This may mean getting up at 5:00 in the morning! That is not the case in sunny Florida, but it is quite common in areas of the country where golf is truly a seasonal game and courses are virtually full any time it does not snow. Depending on the weather, particularly in the summer, you may wish to schedule one of those 2:00 P.M. tee times, after the morning crowd is long gone. Ask the professional or the starter, explain your situation, and accept what advice you get. Consideration of others, even those not in your group, is a part of the game that takes a little more time but adds a lot more class to the experience. Planning can mean the difference between a long-term profitable relationship and a lost business opportunity.

Here are some very simple scenarios that, when handled appropriately, show consideration for others on the course.

Problem 1

You know it is going to be a long round because:

1. You and/or your guest are relatively new golfers.

2. The foursome is an inexperienced group.

Solution 1

Start later in the day and let the starter know the capabilities of the foursome so you don't hold up others. This is just common courtesy, and the other golfers will appreciate it without even knowing what you have done. Additionally, if everyone in your group is an advanced player, the starter may put you ahead of the group in front of you, out of courtesy to you. If that happens, gracefully acknowledge the group that is now behind you. Offer a few words of encouragement, thank the starter for the gesture, and you'll be surprised by the positive attitude adjustment that results. It's like one of those free deposits to the less experienced golfer's emotional bank account.

Problem 2

You know that the round will be short because:

1. Somebody has another time commitment that day, yet nine holes will accomplish the objective.

2. You have only a twosome or a threesome.

3. All you truly need is some one-on-one time, and an hour or two will likely suffice.

Solution 2

Consider starting later in the day so you don't bother groups behind you. The point here is to think about the other golfers, and your game will be more enjoyable, too. Playing a shortened game at a peak period for the course may have prevented some other foursome from being able to get a tee time. If you don't have a foursome you'll play more quickly and may unintentionally push the group in front of you. Remember that a foursome has priority over a threesome, a threesome has priority over a two-some, and a twosome should really try to join another group.

If a guest cannot commit to a particular time, the group is in trouble. You will be forced to meet at the golf course and be at the mercy of the starter. This is *not* recommended, and it's not an example of good organizational skills. But it happens. Golfers plan whole days around the game, knowing that weather is about the only thing that can affect the day. Those who show up without a prearranged tee time can't expect to enjoy the same privileges of those who planned ahead. Our comments are made with the recognition that there are exceptions, but as a general rule, plan ahead, fill your foursome, and schedule the tee time to make maximum use of whatever time is available in your plan for the day. But above all, respect the rules of the club you are playing at as far as twosomes and threesomes are concerned. It is not unusual for resorts and public courses to allow only a full group of four players on the course. This doesn't mean you can't find a game without planning, but if you do, it's pure luck.

Assume there are only two of you. Depending on what time you get to the course, the starter may be able to fit you in quickly. It is always a good idea to call in advance to get some idea of the wait. If you and your playing partner have to wait awhile, then use that time to develop some understanding about your partner's background. It may not be a good idea to focus on business topics unless your playing partner brings it up and initiates the conversation in that direction. Keep in mind that while you may be the one who invited the other person, it is a two-way street with respect to getting to know each other. Your guest may be looking at your manners and mannerisms just as you are observing his. Golf is a funny game. It transcends all age groups, personalities, and types of etiquette—or lack thereof. Generally speaking, what you see is what you get, on the golf course and in the boardroom.

A Business Consultant Talks, Plays, and Breathes Golf

I don't go to a golf course looking for business. The business meeting in the office generally gets around to golf for a few minutes, since it is obvious that pictures of great golf courses on the wall indicate some affinity for the game. Invariably, we talk about getting together for a round later. God made calendars on the computer so they can be easily accessed to schedule rounds of golf weeks into the future. More than a few times a golf game is scheduled before the business meeting is over. We may have a meeting prior to the round, at a nearby restaurant, in the clubhouse, or even at the office. It is often a good idea to bring somebody in the company into the loop, and it helps to ask your guest to bring somebody from his company to fill out the foursome. It is a means of leveraging the entire relationship, and again, in most cases that is what we all want to do.

I Don't Have a Game, What Do I Do?

If you come as a single, without a playing partner, the chances of getting off quickly may be greater. The starter may put you with a group of two or three, or you may be part of a fivesome, if the course allows fivesomes. This brings us to another technique in developing relationships on the course. In this instance you do not have a prearranged playing partner and are playing potluck to some degree. If you happen to be alone (imagine that—just going to a course for the sheer enjoyment of the game!), you may suddenly find that you know nobody within a mile. Nothing wrong with that! Golf can be enjoyed wearing many hats, so to speak. Since you've already planned the day, settle in with the situation and enjoy the whole experience. The suggestions throughout this book will work with a new group, too.

Pat's Story About the Baptist Preacher

Playing golf at the Lake City Country Club was an experience like no other. One of the great things about it was that everybody could play. It doesn't matter whether you have five, six, or seven—I've even seen as much as a ninesome. One day this Baptist preacher from Lake Butler, Florida, down near Starke, showed up and asked if he could join us, and I said, "Sure."

The preacher started out pretty poorly. He hit one left, then hit one right, and finally dumped one in the lake. We had this other guy, a kind of redneck from Lulu, another little town near Lake City, who had missed the introduction. So on the second tee he comes up to the preacher and says, "What's your name?"

The preacher says, "Bob Reynolds."

Then the redneck says, "Bob, you need to change your luck. You need to find yourself a gal and . . ."

I said to the guy from Lulu, "Bob's a preacher."

The guy from Lulu responded with a red face, "Well, it's too late. Nothin' I can do about it now."

On a resort course you will typically find businesspeople from out of town, sometimes couples who are enjoying the chance to get together during a business trip. Private clubs are more likely to present opportunities to find business relationships, but that, in and of itself, should not be the reason to join a particular club. Join a club to play golf and entertain. Play it with appropriate etiquette, and business relationships will inevitably develop, sometimes when you least expect it.

Let's go back to the situation where the golfer is out looking for a game and happens to be paired with a stranger. At this point you are not sure if this individual is someone you want to do business with, and the game was not set up to be a business round anyway. But why not get a little practice on the skills of how to play BusinessLinks. Your playing partner may well be in the same frame of mind. It is appropriate to ask early on what kind of business each of you is in and other general business questions.

At this point etiquette takes the same stance (no pun intended) that it would if you were sitting next to each other on an airplane, a subway, or in a corner cafeteria: start talking. If you find that there is little business chemistry in the air, you may choose to stop with the business questions and play the round. Your objective may now be to get his business card so that you can call him next week to set up another round of golf, but this time with a purpose. Incidentally, a rainproof sandwich baggie in your golf bag with business cards is a nobrainer.

On the other hand, if the conversation looks like it has a good chance of continuing around the business discussion, by all means keep it going. One of the key rules of good telephone etiquette applies here. When the caller finally contacts the person he has been trying to reach, it is always polite to ask if this is a good time to talk, or even indicate that you need ten minutes, and ask if that is convenient for him. Say anything that shows an understanding that some time is needed, and if this is a bad time, say, "Can we reschedule the call?" Most business people appreciate that. If the ego is bigger than the room, then a strikeout is coming anyway. In golf, anticipate when the double bogey may happen. If the gut call is that this is a bad time to bring up business, chances are the gut is right.

But the opposite works, too. Often it is just a casual "Can we talk a little more about your new warehouse?" that will set the conversation in motion. It may solicit an exchange in which you agree to follow up next week after the attorneys have reviewed the contract on that warehouse. A carefully orchestrated inquiry will tell you very quickly when to ask for the sale, so to speak.

9

Equipment

There are specific USGA rules regarding the types and number of clubs a player can have (fourteen clubs, Rule 4-4). You don't have to spend a fortune on equipment, but having the right equipment is important—it shows that you are serious about the game. The many advancements in today's equipment boggles the mind of even a sophisticated golfer, much less a new player. The PGA merchandise shows present hundreds of companies displaying their wares, taking orders, and debuting new golf equipment, accessories, and apparel. The January PGA show in Orlando covers 1.2 million square feet!

So we have a few equipment alternatives. Taking the time to pick the right clubs for your style of play can absolutely affect your score. Line up a session with your PGA professional. You will appreciate his advice when you use your new equipment. In BusinessLinks, looking the part is helpful in building rapport, and first impressions are very important. A quality bag and a good set of clubs are part of the package that reflects your image to your playing partners. Remember that your guest is sizing you up, too! Pocket protectors are geekish in the office, and ratty-looking equipment has the same effect on the golf course. By the way, if you still wear golf shoes with flaps, or penguin shirts with the underarm gussets, put those things back in your '60's and '70's closet.

Be sure to have a good ball mark repair tool and a ball marker. Keep some extras in your bag in case your playing partner needs some. It's a nice gesture, and usually an inexpensive one, to offer your guest a logoed repair tool. It really doesn't matter what kind of ball marker you have as long as it is thin and small. Many clubs offer inexpensive repair tools free, so take advantage of that; it shows you care about the course. Don't forget to repair an extra ball mark while you are leaning over on the green. Another major point on course management: the sand buckets on carts should be full when the round starts and close to empty when it is over. A courteous golfer fixes ball marks, rakes bunkers, and fills divots even when playing alone. It's part of the game's tradition and shows respect for the facilities we all enjoy.

At Least They Haven't Come Up With Fairway Faxes—Yet

Cellular phones and beepers are part of almost every businessperson's standard equipment, but nothing can be more aggravating than having a cell phone ring on the golf course! If you must have your phone with you, set it to the vibrate mode, or bring a beeper. Check it periodically, but leave it in the cart. Only make a call if it's an emergency. Your playing partner is not impressed that you have a cell phone on the course, and it may actually upset the group. There is even a chance that your playing partner may be on the course to get away from civilization! Remember that many clubs do not allow cell phones on the course, just as many private lunch clubs do not permit cellular phones in the dining areas.

Tell the group on the first tee that you may have to take or make an important call that could not be rescheduled, and then do so between the green and the next tee. If you are still on the phone when your partners are ready to hit, be off to the side so your conversation doesn't interrupt the 290-yard drives. Before the end of the last hole, determine if your call may cause undue delay on the course, and be sure your playing partners are okay with your "emergency," because conducting unnecessary business is irritating and slows play. The important point here is to be certain to share whatever interruptions may happen during the round with the group so you don't alienate your playing partners all day long. We know of a very successful businessman who insists on being contacted through his private "priority" line in the office, as well as leaving his cell phone turned on while playing golf. Yet when he answers the phone—in the office or on the course—the comment is "I'll have to get back to you, I'm in a meeting." Why not just leave the phone off and use the administrative assistant instead of a private line? It's one of those idiosyncrasies that irritates his playing partners, and is an example of selfishness.

Dress Codes

Nothing is more embarrassing than greeting your guest, only to see he is wearing clothing unacceptable to the rules of the club. Dress is important, because many clubs have specific, nonnegotiable requirements. The object is to play the part of a conscientious golfer. Tennis shoes, no-collar shirts, blue jeans, tennis shorts, "brown socks with black golf shoes," and generally shabby appearance are not appropriate. At many clubs, sloppy dress may cause embarrassment when the management asks the host to change clothing to comply with club rules. It is truly embarrass-

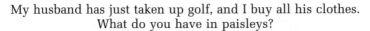

My husband has just taken up golf, and I buy all his clothes.
What do you have in paisleys?

ing to have to ask a guest to go to the pro shop to find a pair of shorts that are not tennis-length, a pair of slacks because shorts are not allowed (this is very rare, but it does happen), or a shirt with a collar because T-shirts are taboo. Check with the pro shop about the dress code to comply with the club rules. Public courses are much less stringent than private ones. Let's face it, a little effort at looking the part can't really harm the relationship you are trying to solidify.

Kids Have Dress Codes Too

We can't neglect comment on dress codes for the younger golfers and how to handle the different kinds of clothing that are seen at the golf courses around the world. In most cases, kids don't want to wear anything but T-shirts (again, no pun intended) and jeans. The vast majority of golf clubs, and certainly almost every private club, require, as a minimum, shirts with collars and shorts which are no more than a few inches above the knee.

The reason is very simple, and it goes back to the tradition of the game, a facet we all want to pass along to the younger generation. The class associated with this game includes a heavy emphasis on looking the part of a real golfer, no matter how our capabilities develop. We don't have to wear knickers and ties, and women don't have to wear the long dresses we see in those old pictures of St. Andrews, but certain attire is just not acceptable. Rarely do we see a staff person at any pro shop who doesn't look the part.

As we share the opportunity to learn the game with new golfers of all ages, we should point out that the dress code is quite simple. Learn whether shorts are allowed, males are to wear shirts with collars, and all men's shirts are to have sleeves. We are not seeing too many golfers out there with shirttails hanging out, and proper dress can be taught to the new golfer, particularly the youngsters who are so willingly taking up the game. New golfers coming into the game can see good examples by watching any professional tournament on television.

We may not be able to play like the professionals, but we can definitely dress like them. We don't mean to imply that our children's wardrobe of jeans and T-shirts are absolutely not allowed on the course, but after a short time, if the club rules don't already insist, the kids will see, by example, not only how to play but how to dress. As the junior clinics are being arranged for your children, check on the rules of dress. It is not a good thing to have to embarrassingly inform your child that you didn't know the rules.

10

The Caddie's Hidden Value

Pat Summerall Recalls an Augusta Experience

I had been at Augusta in 1945 as a caddy. All the regular caddies were in the service, so if you were invited to play you had to bring your own. I was in junior high and a local druggist, Brannon Hill, was invited to play so he took me to Augusta. I caddied three days for 50 cents a bag per round. One day I made a dollar because we went thirty-six holes. Looking back, I had no idea what the day would mean in my memories.

One of the more interesting and unique aspects of golf is that, in spite of the idea that it is mostly an individual sport, it is also a team sport when it comes to the member-guest events, scrambles, and other partner-arranged games. If a golfer has never had the experience of using a caddie, or a runner, as a forecaddie is often called, put the experience on the "to do" list.

We think there are far too few caddies in the world, and it has been a tough row to hoe, or perhaps a tough bunker to rake, for the career caddie. Homer Hemingway, a wonderful friend for many years, is one of the very few folks in the world of golf who has made his living as a caddie. He has been at one club, the Palma Ceia Country Club, in Tampa, Florida, for fifty-seven years. Now we have seen some loyalty in a chosen career, but Homer exemplifies the tradition of the game like no other caddie we could find. So with that in mind, let's go over some basic considerations when a caddie is part of the group.

Who Pays the Caddie?

As a rule, a caddie arrangement is established through the golf shop. Check with the club when you set up the game to determine if it is one of the unusual few that still has caddies. Learn the going rate before the first tee so there are no surprises, and have an understanding with your playing partners who will share the expense, and the services, of the caddie.

In a business golf game, we think it is appropriate to share the expense of the caddie, or even offer to pay for the caddie if you are the guest. Liken it to the restaurant experience when somebody is picking up the tab, for cash, and one of the parties offers to leave the tip. If the caddie is being charged along with the greens fees through the tab in the golf shop, then it is more difficult to extend the offer to pay for the caddie. In most clubs, however, caddies are paid in cash, so at least make the offer to your host somewhere during the last couple of holes. It will be appreciated, and often accepted as a courtesy. Regardless of who reaches in the pocket, be sure some gratuity finds its way to the caddie.

Be on the lookout for the stingy partner who takes advantage of the caddie's skill and knowledge, and then balks on sharing the expense, or agrees to give a tip that is half the normal amount, thus insulting the caddie as well as the others in the group. He is liable to be the same sort of businessperson, so judge the relationship accordingly.

Homer Hemingway Interview

Homer Hemingway has more memories of the golfer wanna-bes and the lazy lackeys than this book has pages. We asked Homer to comment on the subject, and he offered the following words of wisdom.

W.R.: Homer, what is the worst experience you can recall working as a caddie?

H.H.: I can honestly say, I can't think of any bad experiences. Now, I've caddied for all kinds of golfers, and I've seen just about everything you can imagine. I just pay attention, do my job, and quietly laugh to myself when I see some of the things people do. I've caddied for sons who became fathers, and then grandfathers, and now I know their whole families.

W.R.: Who was the first professional golfer you caddied for?

H.H.: Sam Snead in the 1950s at Palma Ceia, when he was in his prime. He already had a green jacket.

W.R.: Do you play much golf?

H.H.: Of course. I used to be a 1 or 2 handicap, but that was years ago. I just enjoy helping other golfers now. I still play once a week, whether I need it or not.

W.R.: What do you think about the future of caddies?

H.H.: I think everyone who starts playing golf as a kid should spend time as a caddie. I've been offered countless opportunities from golfers I met while caddying. I know of several ex-caddie friends who got their start in business through the relationships they developed by caddying. But few clubs offer it anymore, and I really think it's a shame. Personally, I think that all clubs should create a caddie program for the kids during the summer, especially at the inner-city municipal courses. The First Tee Program will be a wonderful way to make a difference for kids who otherwise may never experience this lifetime game. It will be great to see sponsors kick in a few dollars for equipment and lessons. It will also give kids a chance to experience golf, make some money, and just maybe, keep a few out of trouble.

Junior Golf Programs

Junior golf programs around the country often provide willing and able bodies for the laborious tasks of helping with yardages, raking bunkers, offering to get the extra clubs left on the green or tee, and attending the flagsticks. The real opportunity for us, however, is to take a young golfer-caddie under our wings, train him in the sport, let him see what a tremendous thing golf really is, and pay him to learn. More than a few times a great golfer got his start as a caddie. With the younger generation getting into the game, unlimited opportunity exists to positively influence young golfers through their participation in a caddie experience. Show us one young caddie who isn't, generally speaking, a good, wholesome youngster, eager to learn, physically fit, and grateful for the chance to earn a few extra bucks. The industrious student who wants to understand the inside of the sport through the caddie ranks is undoubtedly a leader for tomorrow. So allow us to lecture a little here. Find a caddie, and use him.

The First Tee Program

The First Tee Program, headquartered in Jacksonville, will serve as a model certain to be duplicated worldwide. It will go a long way toward helping our young golf population. The objectives of the First Tee Program include giving inner-city green areas a breath of fresh air by creating golf courses and practice areas in otherwise open, underutilized, or unused public space. Kids who live in those areas will have a place to go to learn this game we all enjoy. While the program is new as we go to press, it has already received the attention of some of the country's major corporations. Companies are giving careful consideration to getting involved at levels of commitment never dreamed about only a few years ago. They see the value of golf and are reviewing how this civic involvement can impact the corporate mission. Improving the game's accessibility to people of every social strata will, over time, make a positive impact on society. That will be a result of teaching, through golf, the values of honesty, sportsmanship, integrity, as well as the key value of self-discipline.

Caddie, Coach, Confidant

Let's go back to the experienced caddie and see how he can be of real help during the game. Begin by asking how long the caddie has been at the course. Chances are good that a caddie can make the difference of a couple of shots in your game! Regardless of what handicap you carry, knowing where a hidden bunker is or if there is a lake around a blind corner can save precious strokes, and ultimately make for a more enjoyable experience.

In every sport, a coach is usually a quick study of a player's prospects. The athlete's demeanor, the physical finesse exhibited, or the lack of finesse, tell a story to the coach or a scout in short order. In any sport, people and teammate skills are all sized up in a short time. The caddie has those same analytical skills, and a good caddie puts them to use by about the third or fourth hole. He knows whether a player should use a seven- or eight-iron to the green, based on the player's already exhibited skill as well as the caddie's knowledge of the course. An experienced caddie can determine if a suggestion of any kind will make any difference at all in the golfer's play. At those courses where caddies add to the aura of the experience, you can believe that they watch the players on the practice green and know at the first tee if interaction with their player may make a difference in the game.

By the way, if you happen to be in a group accompanied by several caddies, count on them having their own wager on the day's game among themselves. A caddie who wants to have a chance to return with the group will keep those wagers to himself, because he will not want to put any additional pressure on the golfer. Trust us—the finer caddies will secretly gamble on your game. Often they are good golfers themselves, so their advice usually comes with some credibility.

When it comes to the green, figure that the caddie has seen virtually every part of the course more times than you can imagine. If you're not certain about a putt, get clarification before you step up to the ball. Then, above all, accept responsibility for whatever happens once you stroke the putt. The caddie didn't hit it, so don't pass the blame. It puts a real damper on the day when a golfer complains that the caddie misread the green, and then doesn't shut up about it for six more holes. Using caddies should speed up the game, so with respect to speed of play, we shouldn't use the caddy as an excuse for a slow, U.S. Open atmosphere in a friendly round of golf.

Assume that everyone is riding in a cart and the caddie is being utilized by a foursome as a runner. Why use a caddie, or in this case, a forecaddie? Well, a forecaddie is already 180 yards down the fairway when you hit, so he can locate the errant shots quicker, which speeds up play. He will also have your putters and drivers ready when you get to the ball, rake the bunkers, fix the divots, repair the ball marks, or grab another beverage at the thirteenth green, which happens to be near the clubhouse. He is also there to clean the clubs throughout the round. He'll have a wet towel to wipe the balls on the green after your ripping approach shot has spun back twelve feet, and he'll also be there to remind the group that it was a six-footer for a 7, not a 6. And he'll even be able to do that with credibility. Homer is a master at that. But fifty-seven years enables him to offer the distance to the green for a playing partner on the other side of the fairway with unbelievable accuracy, and he can read a putt without going behind the ball. He'll recall everybody's shot on every hole and last week's game as well. Homer Hemingway is an exception and a real gentleman whom we're proud to have with us in Tampa. But he is not there to keep score. That task is for the golfer. A prudent caddie doesn't touch a scorecard, lest he record an error and not only catch your wrath, but most likely sacrifice some part of your generous tip.

We Can't Resist a Few Stories About Caddies

We were a group of eight amateurs at Pittsburgh's Oakmont, one of the world's finest and most traditional clubs. It was June 1983, U.S. Open time, so it was hot, around eighty-five degrees. There were four caddies between the groups. Our host member agreed that it didn't matter who took which caddie, so we went along with our assigned "toters." Jamie, our friend and playing partner, who might be 140 pounds soaking wet, was seen walking down the 602-yard twelfth hole carrying his own, extra-large "traveling" bag, while the very experienced, but somewhat frail older caddie marched behind some forty yards carrying nothing but a cup of cold water. What a sight!

Caddies are a different breed. Some talk too much; some say hardly anything. There is a caddie at Pinehurst in North Carolina, a real family man, which he explained to us going down to the first hole. He loved his daughters, all thirteen of them. But that was nothing; his father had twenty-six. We couldn't concentrate for three holes—twenty-six daughters!

There was the caddie at St. Andrews in Scotland whose brogue was impossible to understand. But he would simply hand us the right club and then say, "The line is . . ." and point in the direction we were to aim. It worked. He got a good tip.

The caddie at Gleneagles in Scotland had four kids and had been laid off from one of the automobile plants nearby. He had a college degree, had been out of work for months, and discovered he could do better caddying at Gleneagles. We had a long discussion about union labor, U.S. imports, and the British crown. Can't remember his name, but we definitely remember the experience.

At Orlando's Dubsdread Golf Club, there was a big, no—he was a *huge* fellow named Gus, who was a good mentor and a very knowledgeable caddie. He definitely would show the younger caddies the ropes, so to speak, all the while singing the old song "Mother-in-Law." It seemed like those were the only words he knew, just "mother-in-law," to which he would add, "huh." Then Gus would throw quarters to the line behind the cart barn, more times than not taking a few quarters from the less experienced gambling preteens. He wouldn't tolerate cussing or laziness, but he could read a green, and he taught others as much as he could. It was a learning experience, and one which, when all is said and done, firmly planted lifetime memories.

Caddie stories around the world could fill volumes, and if there is ever a chance to influence some young person to learn the game by serving others, this is a good way. It is another reason why we should take our own children and grandchildren to the golf course anytime we can. We can't put a price on teaching the people skills that every caddie has to learn.

Mulligan

- Plan your event and determine with whom, when, where, and why you'll play.

- Be prepared for coed BusinessLinks.

- Find out your guest's handicap.
- Carefully select the other players in your foursome.
- Determine your ultimate objective.
- Get to know your local pro shop staff to help make the overall experience even better.
- Confirm your game with a note to your guest.
- Offer a choice of tee times, if possible, when inviting your guest.
- Invite others who will add to the experience to fill out the foursome.
- Have the right equipment; it will also help you play better.
- Turn off your cell phone and beeper, or use the vibrate mode.
- First impressions are important, so dress appropriately.
- Consider hiring a caddie. Doing so will make the round more memorable.

Part III
THE ARRIVAL

11

Be Prepared

When I saw what was in his bag, I knew he could play the game, so I mentally prepared for the day.

—COLLEGE COACH TEACHING GAMESMANSHIP TO HIS TEAM

P lanning your day of golf is very important. Arrive at the course early, and be sure to inform the gate guard the name of your guest and what time he will arrive. Pay for everything in advance if you can so that you eliminate any awkward situations. Be sure to invite your guest early enough so that you can hit some balls on the driving range and practice a few putts.

Always Arrive Early and Be Prepared

(BusinessLinks Fourth Commandment)

Make your guest feel welcome. It sets the tone for the day. He knows immediately that you are the host. Arrange to have a cart in advance of your guest's arrival. If you can meet him at his car, then you or one of the club's employees should do so. Obtain a guest locker, and let the attendant know that you have a new face to introduce to the club. It's all part of making the club your guest's home for a few hours. Your focus should be on your guest. Take him into the pro shop and introduce the starter or resident pro. See if he has all the supplies he'll need (balls, glove, tees, coffee, cigar, etc.). There should be a towel on the cart. Take him to the driving range. Have a bucket of balls ready. Spend a few minutes on the practice green. Assuming this is the first time he has played the course, he may not know anyone. (By the way, even though it is appropriate for the host to pay the guest and cart fee, it is not the same with all the supplies. It may not be obvious to a new golfer, but if you are a guest, be prepared to pay for your own water balls!)

Another important item is to ask the starter how the course is playing, the cart rules, and about flag placements. This information will not only help you, it will also help you be a better caddie for your guest. Most of the better resorts have a starter or ranger who spends a couple of minutes explaining the lay of the land, such as cart path rules for the day. This is a good time to ask any questions about the course and its condition. The rangers generally know the history of the course too, so if you have difficulty engaging your guest, here's another person to help break the ice.

Warm-up, Driving Range, and Practice Green

Sometimes you can get an idea of the type of personality you are preparing to play with. The driving range is a great place to find out many things about your playing partner. You can check out his level of skill, and take a look at his bag. Most golfers have mementos from other golf courses they have played. There's probably a club tag representing membership at a local club you know about, or a club out of town. In either case, it serves as a reason to ask the next question, "Tell me about Lone Lake Golf Club." If clubs are arranged in perfect order, with covers for each club, you may be with a perfectionist. By the way, club covers on irons are like that pocket protector on the class nerd. It may protect the sticks, but it takes more time, looks silly, and gives a first impression, like the class nerd, which may not be fair, but unfortunately comes off as a negative.

On the other hand, if there is no club placement order in the bag and there are several different types of clubs, he may be a really good golfer (who chooses to play with clubs he hits with well, regardless of whether they match the rest of the set), or someone who throws his clubs, and the bag simply carries the scarred remains of many sets. We promise, those folks do exist! The skill demonstrated on the driving range should give you good insight.

What About Advice to Your Playing Partners?

A person who has good skills is not likely to be someone looking for a playing lesson. The opposite is true for the person with poor skills. Generally speaking, offering help is good only if you are asked, but don't be afraid to tell your playing partners that your skill level does not quite justify giving tips. It could be a good time to talk to the local pro, who may be consulted for help on that ugly shot that was just hit.

If your playing partner has all the latest equipment, your guest may be serious about his game, or he may have just had a birthday. He may have the swing of a tour player. Unfortunately, he would then be a real exception. It is likely that he plays often, really enjoys the game, and is just as happy to be out on the course as you are and does not care if he shoots 75 or 105. Golf is a classy sport, and most of the golfing public views it that way. Most of us like to look the part, even if we can't play the part. On the other hand, a golfer may look like a million dollars, but the impression on the first tee lasts about three shots. At the end of the day, regardless of his dress and equipment, he has made so many faux pas he may never get another game with the same group!

Teaching Professional Johnnie Jones Talks About Lessons

What I see all too often is a member who comes to me and says he can't seem to shoot any better than his current score no matter how much he practices. So many golfers today are self-taught and have some basic errors in their swing. I tell a golfer that I will be happy to show him the correct way, but it will take some time to get used to the new way of playing and his score may suffer in the meantime. So he takes one lesson, shoots terrible, and decides he would not take two steps back in order to take three steps forward. It's critical to take lessons when you start the game so the fundamentals are learned. It is much harder to relearn anything.

If you have not determined your guest's handicap, ask him on the practice green. Be sure to discuss and agree on the rules before you begin play. For example, agree on what the group will do about mulligans off the first tee, adjusting the bet after the first nine, ready golf, winter rules, and so forth.

Your Tee Time Is Not the Time
You Arrive at the Course

One more comment about the practice area. Try to get to the course early enough to hit a few balls. Some of us are fanatics about hitting thirty balls or more before the game. Others can step up to the first tee, whale away, and surprise the whole group with an accurate shot down the middle. But if you have a guest, chances of enhancing the relationship are better if you arrange the schedule so there is sufficient time to do a little warming up. Become knowledgeable about arrival times, tee times, and whether you can relax for thirty minutes after the game is over. It's just like planning a meeting. Find out how much time you have with your guest. You would be disappointed if, after the round, your guest had to leave because of a prior arrangement and you didn't take the time to obtain this information earlier. You just missed the opportunity to both relax after the game, as well as set the tone for your next meeting.

The practice green is very informal, giving you an opportunity to talk about several things. You can ask a few questions about business to see how your guest responds. You can keep it light and joke around a little, again to gauge his reaction. Finally, you can determine the stakes of the day's game, if this is deemed appropriate. If the whole group gathers on the practice green, small talk about choosing partners allows you to avoid delays on the first tee. If you are unsure of how to begin the small talk, here are a few suggestions:

1. Tell him about your golf clubs, how long have you had them, and whether they have helped your game.

2. Ask about other courses your guest has played, and mention your favorites.

3. Ask what club he belongs to, if any.

4. If you watched the latest golf match on TV, ask your guest if he watched it as well.

Usually, a few questions will get the ball rolling and other areas of interest will soon pop up. In fact, this is a good time to make a point. On crowded courses, there is nothing more aggravating than waiting on the first tee for the group in front to "make the game"—finish the betting and partner arrangements—which could have been done on the practice tee or the putting green. Meanwhile, the prior group is already on the green, you are a half hole behind, and you haven't even been called to the first tee! Discuss if you are going to take any mulligans, or take gimmies on the green, but do it before you step to the first tee.

12

Different Formats

Just the two of us played in the late afternoon and we had
a ball.

—Retired attorney, recruiting for his firm

T here are several formats you can play in BusinessLinks.
You can go out as a twosome and have the undivided
attention of your guest. However, we don't recommend it,
especially if this is the first time you have played with your
guest. You never know how the relationship will develop. You
and your guest may find it a little awkward, especially if one of
you is not a good communicator. You may find yourself trying
to come up with conversation, and suddenly a relaxing time
becomes somewhat stressed for both of you. Or you may be with
a nonstop blabbermouth, and would give almost anything if
someone else were there to listen to his pearls of wisdom.

Occasionally, you may be in a threesome; one of your guests
may have had to drop out at the last minute. Threesomes are fine
and can prove very enjoyable; it is a more intimate situation.
With three people the chances of not finding good conversation
are slim. With a threesome, the only negative is the speed of play.
If the three of you are playing fairly quickly you may find yourself waiting more than normal. If the course is full, you're stuck,
so you might as well take your time and just keep pace with the
group in front.

Recently we learned of a game to play in a threesome that
keeps everyone on their toes. Dave Detone, a member at Winged

Foot, introduced us to "baseball" during an outing at La Quinta's Nicklaus course. Here's how to play. Each hole is worth nine points. You play for a dollar, two dollars, fifty cents, or whatever. With crowds that like to gamble, doubling the back nine can make for a pretty good sense of competition. All bets are based on the net score, so you can play this game with any handicap player, and it gets very interesting as the holes go by. The winner of the hole gets five points, the loser gets a point, and the player in the middle gets three points. If all three players tie the hole, each gets three points. If two players with the low score tie, they get four points each, and the loser gets a single point. If two players tie the hole, but the third had a lower net score, the low score gets five points, the others get two points each. So at all times the total points for each hole add up to nine. Be sure to understand the game, as we think it is one of the best formats we know of, but it only works in a threesome.

Here's a quick tip on cart etiquette in a threesome. When somebody is riding alone, it's easy to be rude by not including the single rider in the conversation, and that is not good BusinessLinks. Be conscious of your situation, and go the extra mile to include the single rider. This sends a message to your guest that you are sensitive about other people around you.

The most typical format, the foursome, creates a multitude of options regarding games, seating, and communication. We have stressed the careful planning of your golf outing. If you are inviting someone you are hoping to do business with and it's the first time you have played golf with him or her, then it's very important who fills out the foursome. The key is to know as much about your guest as possible so that you might invite other players to complement you or your guest. Therefore, understanding different personalities is critical.

A Manufacturer's Rep Doing Business With an Aussie

One of the best experiences I had with business golf occurred when I didn't even ride with my guest. I knew that he was from Australia, and that he had just moved to the United States. I was trying to develop a business relationship with him because his company provided a particular item that I needed for my clients, and I wanted to get the best price that I could. I asked a guy from my club—he was also from Australia—if he would join us. He was delighted. I decided to put my guest and the member from Australia together in the same cart. Well, they hit it off and I hardly had a chance to talk to my guest throughout the whole round. He must have had a great time, because the following week when I called him for pricing, he gave me the product four points under the going rate. You must understand, I'm talking about a savings of thousands and thousands of dollars based on the volume I was dealing with. How's that for a day on the course? By the way, we play together several times a year now, and he's become a good friend.

Here's Another Example of How to Set Up a Game

You are a stockbroker interested in developing a relationship with a CPA you recently met who plays golf. You discovered that the CPA specializes in the medical area, and he has quite a reputation in estate planning. You made several calls to physicians you know who play golf. You are acquainted with a physician who is also new to the area, who expressed an interest in another accounting firm. You are also aware that the CPA has a 33 handicap and both you and the doctor have 10 handicaps. You decide to invite a respected 26-handicap attorney in town who specializes in estate planning. Then you call both the doctor and attorney to get two or three dates that they can commit to for a round of golf. Finally you call the CPA and make it happen.

This may involve several phone calls and probably more time than you thought it would take to orchestrate. But look what you have accomplished! You have developed a scenario so that everyone in the foursome can benefit, especially the CPA with whom you are trying to establish that referral relationship. The key is to think about what your guests would appreciate and how they might benefit from this round of BusinessLinks. In other words, if you focus on your guests' needs and take yourself out of the picture, the chances of developing a solid long-term relationship with your target guest will almost always work.

Play in a Team Format When Appropriate

(BusinessLinks Fifth Commandment)

Depending on the course you are playing and how crowded it is, you may be able to play with a fivesome. Usually this format is permitted at private clubs when conditions are favorable. You will find the opportunity to wager and have a great time with several players. There are numerous industry association and charity tournaments that are set up as team matches. In some cases, one team may have as many as eight players all playing together. This format is called a scramble. The players select the best shot from the group, and play continues from that spot, and this continues until the hole is finished. The scores are typically very low and in most cases well under par. While there is usually heavy competitive spirit, the format produces one of the most fun kinds of golf you can experience, especially if everyone knows each other. If you are not playing in four or five scrambles every year for charity, you're missing a great opportunity for BusinessLinks, as well as a chance to contribute to good causes.

Inviting someone with whom you would like to do business to a charity tournament can be another way to develop a good relationship. But be sure the person you invite can play golf!

Nothing can be more frustrating than inviting someone for the first time who does not have enough skill at the game to play in a tournament. Instead of showing your guest a good time, you may have created an unpleasant experience. Winning or losing is not the issue. Rather, you must be aware of the pressure your guest feels when he or she is not able to contribute to the team. Inviting someone with whom you would like to do business to a charity tournament can be another way to develop a good relationship. But be sure the person you invite can play the game!

Different formats provide for different opportunities. The key is simple. Do a little research, find out what your guest likes, his handicap, the last time he played, if there are complementary business associates that may lend leverage to the outing, and then orchestrate it to benefit all parties.

13

Games, Scams, Jokes, and Gambling

We believe that big-dollar gambling is not conducive to BusinessLinks. Large-scale bets or hustling games belong in a different venue. They typically are played by golfers who gamble big consistently and who are very aware of their ability to play under that type of pressure. At both extremes, an understanding of gambling is important.

Most golfers like some form of wager just to keep the competitive juices flowing. There is really no magic answer to how or how much to wager, but a review of the parameters is in order.

Start with a friendly, inexpensive game. You can gamble on the golf course and still do business, if you're careful. We have already explained how important it is to establish everyone's handicap before the game begins, but the purpose of BusinessLinks betting is to make the game more fun. Betting adds another element to the game, and for most of us (assuming the wager is not too high) it adds excitement. It's true that there are many golfers who find golf exciting enough without the additional pressure of betting, but for those who want that added element, there are plenty of golfers who share a thirst for swapping dollars at the nineteenth hole.

Mickey Mantle Had Many Games With Pat

He loved to bet. He would bet on everything. There were always so many bets that you just never knew what was at stake. When you got through he'd tell you how much you had lost.

An important step in the outing is finding the betting threshold. Some prefer not to bet or bet for as little as a quarter per hole. If you are playing with someone who likes to wager, the lowest wager you will likely find in a first-time business development game is $1 to $10 per bet, or a $1 to $10 Nassau. The Nassau bet consists of separate wagers for the front nine, the back nine, and the overall eighteen-hole game. It is very common in social and business golf because it gives the players a chance to get even on the back nine if the front nine has been a disaster. It also rewards the players who have been consistent all day long by giving them a chance to win the overall game. Many clubs and public courses have the regular gambling crowd, and it is seldom that the new guest is placed in an uncomfortable setting, but it does happen. Those games typically find hundreds of dollars changing hands at the end of the day, so it is important to know what you are getting into before you tee up.

There will be times when you are playing with someone for the first time and he may not have an established handicap, or he tells you a handicap level that gives him an unfair advantage. It's ironic that when you're talking to someone casually about golf and you're not on the course, more often than not when you inquire about his handicap, he answers with one lower than it really is. Then when you get to the course to establish the handicaps for betting, the same person's handicap goes up! The point is: know your handicap and be prepared to occasionally be taken for a ride.

Establish your handicaps before you enter into any bet. Remember, calculating your handicaps by the USGA rules isn't that difficult. In order to accurately determine a handicap you should use the "slope rating," which takes into consideration the difficulty of all rated courses. One course may have a slope rating of 141, while another might have a rating of 137. The higher the number, the tougher the course. The way you determine an accurate handicap is to multiply the slope rating of the course by your handicap and then divide the result by the USGA standard slope rating of 113. Now you have the accurate handicap. If you need some help on that, see your pro, or ask your accountant!

In BusinessLinks wagering, it's interesting to see how your guest acts under this added element of pressure in the round. You may find that an entirely new personality appears. With the added excitement or pressure of betting, some golfers become very intense and extremely competitive. These same people may go through wide mood swings, depending on whether or not they are winning or losing. Obviously, this can tell you a lot about the way that person may react in a business setting, and ultimately gives an indication about whether you want to do any kind of business transaction at all.

When inviting a guest to play, ask about his handicap when you call to set up the game. Then choose two other players with similar or complementary handicaps. If this is the first time you have played with your guest, team together. Play your heart out to win the game, but wherever possible let your guest win a hole.

For example, if each of you has a five-footer to win a hole for your team, suggest that the guest make it first, then you can play. If he makes it, the team has won and your playing partner feels great. If the two of you win, brag about your accomplishment. One of our friends, a scratch golfer, has more trophies than he can count. In a two-man tournament, this excellent golfer will pick up his own ten-foot birdie putt if his playing partner is already in with a birdie, even if it is a net birdie. He will simply comment that this is a team event, and individual scores don't matter. That says volumes for putting a guest first! Make him feel good. It's important to keep your guest in his element. If he likes to wager, then set it up. If he doesn't, forget it.

BusinessLinks Recommends Match Play

To make the guest and the group comfortable, determine what tees the group usually plays. If your guest normally plays the white tees and you normally play from blues, there's nothing odd about playing the white tees. The point is to be together throughout the round. If you change from your normal tees, then adjust the bet to make it more even. Adjusting the bet to make it more fair is somewhat subjective. You should consider the following:

1. Who is the better player?

2. Is it your home course?

3. Is there a substantial difference between tee markers such that it really requires an adjustment?

4. Do the other players agree with the adjustment?

Remember, it's not who wins that really counts in a business golf game, so don't get carried away with the adjustment issues. When adjusting handicaps based on playing different tees, you might consider giving your guest one or two strokes per side, assuming you are moving from the blues to the whites and that you are a better player.

If this is the first time that you have played with your guest, match play is a simple way to wager. In fact, it is the way most business golf is played. In match play, each hole can be a new bet. If you completely blow one hole, you can redeem yourself on the next. This keeps the extent of losing or winning to a minimum, nobody gets hurt, and the bucks usually just get swapped at the end of the day.

Play for a Dime? This Just In From a Surprised Pat Summerall

I was playing golf in Jacksonville many years ago with a bunch of guys I did not know very well. We got up to the first tee and I said, "How much are we playing for?"

Somebody said, "Let's play for a dime."

Another guy said, "No, let's make it a quarter."

So they kept talking and agreed to play something called Dime, Quarter, Dollar, which sounded harmless enough, although I was a little confused.

We got to the ninth hole, and I asked the guy keeping score, "How are we doing?"

He said, "You're down eighteen hundred dollars."

I said, "What?"

"Yeah, a dime is a hundred, a quarter is two-fifty, and a buck is a thousand."

Needless to say, I lost a lot more than I had planned. Ever since then, I haven't hesitated to make sure I understand exactly what the bet is.

So, you say your handicap is 8. Let's flip a coin to make
the round interesting. Heads for $250 a hole, tails for $500.

What do you do when the bet has been agreed to and it
rains, or someone is injured before the match is finished? Do you
cancel all bets? The person who is winning may not accept that
arrrangement. He may prefer to let the bets be determined by the
holes actually played. Again, establish the rules before the first
ball is hit, and if it's just a friendly business golf game, what difference does it make? Our experience shows that it's best just to
cancel all bets if a problem of any type comes up during the
game. It's just not worth fussing over if one of the golfers has an
issue, or if Mother Nature brings in the elements.

When establishing the rules of the game, be sure to consider
gimmies. Again, in BusinessLinks the idea is to have a relaxed,
enjoyable time. Recommending gimmies (within the leather of the
putter) might be a good idea just to avoid the yips (inadvertent
misstrokes or short putts that don't get anywhere near the hole)
with short putts. This, of course, is an advantage for the yippers!

One of the most common games played in a foursome is
called "best ball." A foursome is broken up into two teams. Each
team takes the best score of the two players. If team one scores a

4 by one of the players and the other scores a 5, then they take the best score (4) for that hole.

In Nassau format, you play the front nine, the back nine, and eighteen holes as three separate bets. There are many different ways you can play it. The most common is a "two-down press." In this game, if one team loses two holes on the front side before the ninth hole, they start a new bet on the same nine holes to try to get even. Many golfers play "greenies" (closest to the pin on par threes), "sandies" (up and down from the bunker), "barkies" (hitting a tree and still making par—an idea first heard about from a prominent 21-handicap insurance agent who will bet almost anything with anyone anywhere), or "polies" (making a par putt that is at least as long as the flagstick). That last one was born, we think, in Corbin, Kentucky, just outside the Pepsi-Cola facility. These betting scenarios, commonly referred to as "junk," make for a lot of fun between holes, and typically create a healthy, lively atmosphere for the game.

Monkeying Around in Golf?

Animals. I'm talking about a gorilla, snake, frog, and a camel. The gorilla is a golfer that hits it out-of-bounds, the snake is a three-putt, the frog hits it in the water, and the camel puts it in the sand. This is a good game to play with clients, because it's a great deal of fun and nobody can get hurt by losing a lot of money. It's up to the golfer to pass on his animal to the other golfer. We pass out all the animals on the first tee so that each of us has one. Then, if I'm the first person to hit it in the sand, I have to take the camel. However, if on the second hole someone else hits it in the sand, then it's up to me to pass the camel to that person. If I forget to pass my camel on the hole where the other golfer hits the sand, then I have to keep it until someone else hits the sand. The same goes for the other animals. At the end of the round, the person who is holding any animals has to pay everyone else one dollar, or five dollars, or buy the drinks, or lunch, or whatever.

Nonbusiness-Building Gambling

The purpose of this section on gambling is to recognize the dos and don'ts of heavy gambling. Inevitably you will come across someone who really enjoys gambling and wants to play for serious money, and you may be trying to develop a potential business relationship.

Heavy gambling is not conducive to building business relationships unless you really know the person you are gambling with. True, there are certain people who gamble big and who would be insulted if they were invited to play without a sizable bet. But you don't want to find yourself out of your element or say adios to your wallet. A little up-front research can go a long way toward making the day enjoyable, regardless of the wager amounts.

Play in Your Own Comfort Zone!

In large gambling games there are many things to be cautious about. Golfers who gamble for large amounts of money are often looking for someone new to hustle. Remember to play in your own comfort zone. Every golfer has a threshold dollar amount to lose before it gets uncomfortable. That's not to say that anyone likes to lose, but gamblers know that they can't always win, so they stay within a dollar amount they can handle. That amount can vary from as little as a few hundred dollars to thousands. It's important that no one talks you out of your comfort zone or the dollar amount you are willing to lose.

If you end up playing for more than you're comfortable with, several things will happen. First, there is pressure. When you are caught in this situation you find that hard shots you are normally confident with become much harder. You may find that you lose the feel or confidence in your putting. Or you may become much more excited than you normally are when you miss a shot, which will affect the rest of your game. Soon you are out of your element, and you lose.

What's interesting is that you don't necessarily have to wager big dollars to get out of your element. So many times we catch ourselves reacting to the people we are playing with or to the

tournament we are in. The key is to play your game and not try
to play out of your game. Remember the following:

1. In tournament play it's not smart golf to try to outplay your
   own abilities (e.g., hitting the ball farther, trying to force hard
   or unrealistic shots, taking additional risks).

2. Don't try to play up to the better player on your team if it
   puts undue pressure on you and if it takes away from the
   enjoyment of the game.

3. If you are the best player on your team, don't try to play
   beyond your capabilities.

4. Whatever your skill level is, play within it.

This brings us to the argument about which is harder, the
physical or the mental side of golf. Golf can be more proactive
than reactive. In other sports, like tennis, football, or soccer, athletes tend to be more reactive. In golf you have an extraordinary
amount of time to think before shots. Most of the time you can
determine whether you are mentally up or down. If you are mentally down, it will affect your game negatively. Maybe you didn't
get enough sleep the night before, or family or business problems
are on your mind. Whatever the problem, it will surely follow
you on the golf course, especially if you are gambling. If you're
going to gamble big and are not in tip-top shape, be prepared to
lose. The game is set at the first tee, so be prepared to live with
the decision to gamble for eighteen holes.

Watch Out for Scams

One of the biggest scams is the traveling threesome. One of the
golfers in the group will ask for or find someone who likes to
gamble (usually on a municipal course) and ask him to join the
group. They will act as though they don't know each other. One of
them will suggest that everyone play Robins. Robins is the game
in which you play every three holes. On the first tee, then the
fourth, seventh, etc., you throw the balls up in the air. The two
balls that land closest together play together, and you switch part-

ners. If they can get you to play for $50 robins or more, you're going to lose a good deal of money. You may be able to beat their best ball, but your partner won't help you. It gets worse; they might want to play low ball, low total. Low total is when you count both scores of the twosome, plus the low ball. You might make a three, a birdie on a par four, while your partner dubs a couple of shots, chili dips one in the bunker, and ends up taking about an eight. So now you've got three and eight—eleven. All the other team has to do is make two bogies—five and five. But they make ten, so you win the low ball, but they win the low total, so there is no action on that hole. They can control the entire round. People have five-putted a green to keep from winning.

A golfer who throws and breaks his clubs, curses at himself, or calls himself names when he misses a putt is the same player who will lose all his money before the day is over. We get just as upset when we miss a putt as he does, but we grin about it. We don't want him to know that it upsets us; that is the worst thing we can do. But sometimes when a group is four or five holes into the match, personality starts showing in a negative way, as a result of the match not meeting the expectations of the hot-tempered playing partner who thinks he's a 10 handicap. He makes a bet based on that handicap and finds himself headed for 90. His demeanor changes, clubs fly, foul mouths curse the course, the weather, or the ex-spouse. Then the day, which started as a great outing, turns sour quickly. The pressure of the wager accentuates the negative attitude, and all of a sudden the whole group has a grim outlook on life. What do you do in this situation? Consider fishing? Quit? Have another beer?

What about just taking a breather, thinking about it, realize that you have the rest of the day to enjoy, and maybe offer some encouraging words to the playing partner who is suffering from a sure case of immaturity. One certainty is that it will be the last time it happens, because Mr. Sourgrapes won't be invited again. Sometimes just canceling the bet is worth it. Golf is too much fun to have a dose of negativism ruin the day for the entire group.

There are many golfers who can't control themselves when it comes to gambling; they want to gamble for more than they can afford to lose. It's like being an alcoholic. They keep thinking that they will win the big one or win more than they lose. These same people keep trying to win. They think they can keep friends and keep pressing and keep trying to get even. They are called money chasers, and they are the biggest losers of all. They will do it whether they are playing gin, golf, or when they go to Las Vegas. They won't quit when they're losing. As the old Kenny Rogers song goes, when the cards are running against you, "You've got to know when to hold 'em, and know when to fold 'em."

Golfers have to understand that we are only human, and everybody chokes. But how we handle the situation has a whole lot to do with how successful we are at gambling. In gambling, we have an advantage when playing with someone who has a big ego and says he never chokes. He winds up being the golfer who gags the most, especially when you casually bring it up. Usually that happens with a short pitch shot that takes a lot of finesse and concentration. Or maybe on a tight par 4 with out of bounds. Choking and lack of concentration go together.

If you're going to gamble with someone you don't know, one of the important things to observe is how he handles his short chip shots and how he putts. This will tell you a lot about the person. If he hits those two shots well, then you are in for a tough round. He's not going to lose it; you're going to have to win it. So it becomes strictly a mental game, which may have very little to do with your golfing ability. When you get into this kind of a game, it's how you handle your mind and your temper that separates the winners from the losers. If you find yourself in a game where the dollar amount involved has you out of your comfort zone, you need to be able to focus on something that will keep your mind off the consequences of the bets. Setting up bets can be an integral part of the experience and can make the game more exciting, but if you do wager, be humble at winning and graceful at losing. For some additional insight on gamesmanship issues, pick up *Combat Golf,* by Captain Bruce Olstein. It is a lively treatise on more of those little nuances of the sport. He takes a different angle than we do, but it is very entertaining.

Good, Bad, and Practical Jokes

If you can't take a joke, then don't play golf! From time to time we have all played a round that was a joke. No one plays the game perfectly. We are focusing on effective business relationship building, no matter what level of play we exhibit. We shouldn't take ourselves too seriously on the golf course, especially during a round of BusinessLinks. On the other hand, we need to understand the individuals we are playing with.

Regardless of the group's personalities, having fun normally includes a joke or two. Telling a good story is not hard, assuming you can repeat it with some measure of skill. Practicing will help in your delivery, and the more you practice the more comfortable you will become. You can find hundreds of jokes in bookstores, or on the Internet. Find jokes that are clean, and some you personally like. If you like them, then typically you will tell them better. However, no matter how much you like the joke, not everyone will. Don't worry! Tell another. It's not comedy hour, but it is supposed to be fun, so join the party. Timing is important here, too. Don't start a five-minute story and hold up play.

Of course, there are some of us who are not comfortable telling stories. That's O.K., too. If you are uncomfortable telling jokes, then don't, just play golf. Be yourself and try to make your guest feel as good as possible. If you try to act like someone other than yourself, it's instantly recognized—and worse than telling a bad joke!

We have a friend in Alabama in the restaurant business who can't keep a straight face to save his life. Roy is more fun to play with than anyone we know, and he plays a decent game. He has the monkey puppet head cover, which inevitably, somewhere in the round, works into one of his jokes, several of which are really crude and really funny, but are not offensive because of the way the guy tells the story. It's a special talent, but Roy says he's going to keep his day job. Telling jokes nonstop for about four hours wears everyone out, but he manages to do a fair amount of business golf as well. It is all in the style, and in the atmosphere we create for our playing partners. Understand that our personality shows vividly on the golf course. And, to a great extent, more so on the golf course than anywhere else, your guest sees everything you do. He observes how we react when we hit a good or bad shot, if we improve our lie or if we try to go overboard in showing him a good time. He sees the real you. So, the rule of thumb is simple. Always play by the rules and have fun.

There are all kinds of practical jokes you can play on your

guest. Practical jokes are different from telling jokes. A practical joke is usually played at someone else's expense. While some can be hilarious for the spectators, they can be embarrassing and maddening to the person at the butt end of the joke. The rule of thumb is not to play practical jokes on anyone unless you have already established a good relationship. Otherwise, you're rude. Most of us have seen the chalk ball that explodes on impact, or the weighted ball that you can't putt straight with. Those are fairly tame; they get worse from there.

Snake! A Tale From a Colorado Comic

I'll never forget the time we were playing two foursomes. We were the first foursome and when we came to the tenth green we saw a small harmless garden snake. My partner picked it up and after we holed out he put it in the cup. Then we waited for the next group to come up. The first person that holed out went to pick up his ball and almost had a heart attack. We never laughed so hard in our lives!

Mulligan

- Get to the course early to plan for your guest's arrival.

- Be sure to invite your guest early enough to warm up, and know if the nineteenth hole is going to be part of the day.

- Think of several opening questions that you can ask your guest in order to get the conversation moving.

- Leave the teaching lesson to the teaching professionals.

- If your guest likes to gamble, make the game inexpensive.

- Consider match play as an option when offering to gamble.

- Establish *all* the rules before you tee off.

- Know several nonoffensive jokes.

- Don't play practical jokes on your guest unless you have an established relationship.

Part IV

PLAYING THE GAME

14

On the Tee

There are many golfers who enjoy the game and successfully do business around golf without the constraints of the USGA rules. But if they are truly successful building those business relationships, in all probability they do a great job of establishing the parameters on the first tee. The problem that can arise if you don't play by the rules (agreed to on the first tee) or use a specific format (such as moving the ball on the fairway—"winter rules"), is that you become used to that loose format. Then when it comes time to playing by the rules you will inevitably play worse. If you post your score using your loose format, then your handicap becomes a liability instead of an equalizing factor.

It really doesn't matter with whom you are paired; the same rules of etiquette apply. The argument of whether or not it is appropriate to bend the rules is clear. Rules are rules. Generally speaking, they are not meant to be broken. But in games that are either hastily put together or when there are no specific relationships that are being "worked," it is not unusual to ignore even some of the basic rules, *assuming that is agreed to on the first tee.* The important issue here is to have an understanding with those with whom you are playing that this is being considered a practice game, or just a "fun game." That's okay, and nobody will be offended. It eliminates all potential problems.

Establish the Rules Before the First Ball Is Hit

(BusinessLinks Sixth Commandment)

Most golfers who practice BusinessLinks follow the rules and etiquette set by the USGA and the local club. Golfers who do not know the rules appreciate a person who does, as long as the knowledge doesn't result in "rules intimidation." In fact, if your guest is substantially better than you are, he will be impressed that you follow the rules perfectly. Again, agree on any rules exceptions on the first tee.

Be sure to establish your handicaps before you enter into a bet. Not everyone you play with will have an established handicap. That's O.K.; just use one they think would best represent their game. Most golfers are honest and the handicap they choose will typically be accurate. If they are sandbagging you by stating they have a handicap that is higher than reality, you will find out soon enough, and may decide doing business with this golfer is more of a gamble than it's worth.

Try Not to Be Judge and Jury

Golf is the only sport that is self-policing. It was established based on integrity, honesty, and ethics. That's why it's the only sport that really shows a person's true personality. Mistakes will happen. Keep in mind that you are not the judge and jury. The key is how the perpetrator deals with the mistake. Does he acknowledge the mistake in a humble manner, or refuse to accept the error and become defensive? Golf tells you a lot about a person. Sometimes we just have to let a "mistake" go by, even if it means losing the hole unfairly. Remember, this is supposed to be fun, not work, so keep it light.

Some golfers make their own rules. Here's a set of rules, which we do not recommend, used by an imaginary Midwest foursome. Enjoy the laughs.

1. On beginning play, as many balls as may be required to obtain a satisfactory result may be played from the first tee. Everyone recognizes a good player needs to loosen up but does not have enough time for the practice tee.

2. A ball sliced or hooked into the rough shall be lifted and placed in the fairway at a point equal to the distance it carried or rolled in the rough. Such veering to the right or left frequently results from friction between the face of the club and the cover of the ball, and the player should not be penalized for erratic behavior of the ball resulting from such uncontrollable mechanical phenomena.

3. A ball hitting a tree shall be deemed not to have hit the tree. Hitting a tree is simply bad luck and has no place in a scientific game like golf. The player should estimate the distance the ball would have traveled if it had not struck the tree and play the ball from there, preferably from atop a nice tuft of grass.

4. There shall be no such thing as a lost ball. The missing ball is on or near the course somewhere and eventually will be found and pocketed by someone else. It, thus, becomes a stolen ball, and the player should not compound the felony by charging himself with a penalty stroke.

5. When playing from the sand trap, a ball which does not clear the trap on being struck may be hit again on the roll without counting an extra stroke. In no case will more than two strokes be counted in playing from the sand trap, since it is only reasonable to assume that if the player had time to concentrate on the shot, instead of hurrying it so as not to delay his playing partners, he would be out in two strokes anyway.

6. If a putt passes over the hole without dropping, it is deemed to have dropped. The law of gravity holds that any object attempting to maintain a position in the atmosphere without something to support it must fall down. The law of gravity supercedes the laws of golf.

7. The same thing goes for a ball that stops at the lip of the cup and hangs defying the law of gravity. You cannot defy gravity!

8. The same thing holds true for a ball that rims the cup. A ball should not go sideways. This violates the law of physics.

9. A putt that stops close enough to the cup to inspire such comments as "You could blow it in," may be blown in. This rule does not apply if the ball is more than three inches from the hole because no one wants to make a travesty of the game.

Honors

First Tee Nerves, Not When You Are Pat's Guest!

Isn't it awful to start out with a one-hundred-foot tee shot? You start off in a bad mood, with a bad score; it destroys the purpose. So around here they have something called "hit it 'til you're happy." Just keep going until you get one in play that you like. I love that rule!

What can you do to relax your guest and get off the first tee in good shape? BusinessLinks recommends that instead of flipping a coin to see who goes first, offer your guest the honor. This is more etiquette-related—a courteous suggestion that your guest play first, at least on the first hole. Don't be concerned with who tees off first on other holes. The rules state that the person with the lowest score tees off first, so if you follow the rules, the first tee is the only place where honor is an issue. A courteous host gives the honor to the guest on the first tee.

One circumstance that inevitably happens on the first tee, and it happens to the best of us, is fear—taking that first swing in front of everyone. Even with a mulligan, most of us feel butterflies, or that sinking feeling of making a fool out of ourselves by duck-hooking the first drive, or topping the ball. Even with a mulligan, if the first shot goes bad, then there is more pressure to hit the second ball well. Golfers who have played any length of time will testify that otherwise calm demeanors present a surprise appearance as a different, sometimes ugly first-tee personality as a result of a failed effort off the tee.

Here's another thought on who should hit first, mostly applicable to events like scrambles when players on the tee have very different levels of skill. Golf can be very intimidating, even to excellent golfers. So a higher-handicap player may wish to hit first, or may be asked to hit first—just to get the ball in play—and that gets him "into the game," and makes him feel more like a part of the team. The golfer who can make his higher-handicap playing partner feel comfortable is miles ahead of the arrogant low-handicapper who intimidates the rest of the group. The idea is that a better golfer will typically hit the ball better and farther, and it can be intimidating to the higher-handicap player if he or she has to hit after the better player. The higher-handicap player instinctively will try to hit the ball as far as the better player, thus overcompensating and resulting in a poor shot.

First Drive and Mulligans

When you are on the tee, take the initiative to tell your guest the best place to drive the ball (assuming he has never played the course before). Point out what to look for, anything you may know that would be helpful. This is all just part of making the group more comfortable to begin the round. If your guest hits a bad shot, take the initiative and suggest a mulligan. Get him off to a good start.

There are really only two things that happen off the first tee. Your playing partner either hits a good shot or a bad one. If he hits a good shot, congratulate him. Don't go overboard, but throw a compliment at him. Conservatism rules. What do you do if he hits his ball out of bounds on his mulligan? Most friendly games allow the golfer to play the first ball, as long as it is in bounds. Every course has its own rule on this one, but in any event, the point is to get off to a decent start.

Obviously, that is not the case in a serious game with a better golf group, and it is not the case in tournament play. Watch closely where the ball flies if it's going out. Then, to encourage faster play, have your guest hit a provisional ball from the tee box. If he hits it out again, you might suggest that he hit another ball from the fairway, next to yours, just for practice, near where he hit the ball out-of-bounds. At this point he has hit three balls out-of-bounds and, for all practical purposes, is probably out of the hole.

Be careful how you suggest that he "pick up." Do it lightly. Some personalities may take offense at the suggestion. We don't see too many purists out there, but there are a few. If the game is being played under match play format, the next hole is a new game!

On the other hand, if you hit the ball out-of-bounds, maybe you just forget it. Hit the provisional shot, and assume the first shot is a lost cause. Don't take much time to look for your ball (assuming you can't readily see it). Take your lumps and continue the game. The objective is to speed up play. These are the principles of course management.

Remember, if you are having trouble on any particular hole (or several holes for that matter) and you are already at triple bogey without being on the green, pick up your ball. This is a BusinessLinks round, so you're not playing golf to score.

President Gerald Ford Plays With Pat and Eight Others

The thing that stands out with President Ford is that you never lose any balls. You've got eight secret service people who go wherever he goes, so instead of one or two people looking, you've got eight or nine. What a nice man, and what a tremendous love of the game. He's eighty-four years old and still plays at a competitive level. He swims five miles every day, and a big reason he does that is so he can still play golf.

A Small Bucket

Some courses don't have a driving range to practice on before you begin play. And often there just isn't time to warm-up prior to the round, especially if it is one of those midweek games and the group hits the first tee still in the office mode. So mulligans on the first tee should be the rule of the day. A Tampa real estate appraiser-developer and a scratch golfer refers to this as a small bucket; the rest of us call it a mulligan. Other than at peak periods, most courses don't mind first-tee mulligans. It's also a helpful way to break the ice in a new relationship when things may be a little tense.

Use "Jitterfix" on the First Tee When Possible

(BusinessLinks Seventh Commandment)

This idea is another suggestion in a less serious game. Your foursome is divided into two teams: you and your guest, and the other two players. One option that can help relieve the pressure for everyone, and this makes it fun, is to play the "jitterfix" on the first tee: (1) everyone can take a mulligan if needed; (2) each team plays their best ball; and (3) both players hit the second shot from the same spot. This does not guarantee a good mulligan shot, but the team has four chances to hit the fairway! Allow your guest to hit first. If he has the first-tee jitters and hits poorly, he can look to the jitterfix for help, and everyone leaves the first-tee smiling.

15

On the Fairway

W hat should you do when you find that your playing partner's ball is directly behind a tree, bush, log, rock, or immovable object? (Rule 28. Ball Unplayable.) Be prepared to give advice to your guest as to the rules of play. Did you know that, under Rule 28-c, after you take a penalty stroke, you can move your ball back away from the pin as far as you want, except in a bunker? Be sure you know Rule 28-a, -b, and -c. This particular rule comes into play often, and many golfers are not familiar with it, so they miss chances to use it to their advantage.

Keep a Copy of the USGA Rule Book in Your Bag

(BusinessLinks Eighth Commandment)

Out of Bounds or an Unplayable Lie?
Here are the Official Rules

"USGA Rule 27-1. If the ball is assumed out of bounds, the player shall play a ball, under penalty of stroke, as nearly as possible at the spot from which the original ball was last played."

"USGA Rule 28, ball unplayable. The player may declare his ball unplayable at any place on the course except when the ball is in a water hazard. Under penalty of one stroke: (a) play a ball as nearly as possible at the spot from which the original ball was last played; or (b) drop a ball within two club-lengths of the spot where the ball lay, but not nearer the hole; or (c) drop a ball behind the point where the ball lays, keeping that point directly between the hole and the spot on which the ball is dropped, with no limit to how far behind that point the ball may be dropped." Pay close attention to every shot and putt your guest makes. Most people like the attention, regardless of their playing ability. We all like the fact that someone is watching our shots. It's courtesy to do so.

When searching for a lost ball, find it quickly. Don't waste time talking to the other players who hit in the fairway. Give you and your partner about ninety seconds, and if two of you can't find it, suggest you move on. If your guest insists on looking further, allow another ninety seconds or so. USGA rules permit up to five minutes. BusinessLinks tries to promote a little faster play. Obviously, if you are waiting on the group in front of you, take the allowable time, but don't overdo it.

Lanny Wadkins Doesn't Give Pat Much Time

Playing with Lanny is an experience with speed. When you get to the ball, you hit it. You'd better think about what club you're going to use while you're getting to the ball. As soon as you get to the ball, you hit it—no practice swings. Even announcing Lanny is a challenge, he is so fast.

Always "Pick Up" When Appropriate

(BusinessLinks Ninth Commandment)

If you find that you are spending the full five minutes looking for a ball, consider telling the group behind you to play through. First, mention this idea to your own players. You will be surprised at how most golfers will resume faster play rather than let the next group play through. It's important to keep control of the round. If there is a hole open in front of you and you know your group can't catch up, regardless of what your guest thinks, you should allow the group behind you to play through, assuming your group is being pressed by those behind you. This is one of those basic golf etiquette mandates. It's also one that is tough to enforce when there are strong personalities in the group.

Single and Alone

A single player has no standing on the course and should give way to all other players in a group, whether it is a twosome, threesome, or foursome. The common courtesy of not holding up a group behind has to be considered, but on a course that is full, remember that a foursome has priority, then a threesome, then a twosome. This is why many resorts and public courses require a full group.

Who Hits First on the Fairway

If your ball is almost the same distance from the hole as your guest's, go to your guest's ball first. Again, this is just common courtesy. It's like opening the door to the restaurant for your guests. Being courteous helps set the stage for your business relationship.

Keep the cart at least a few yards away from the golfer addressing the ball. If the sun produces a shadow, move farther away.

Hazards and Bunkers

If you think of yourself as a caddie it will go a long way in the relationship with your guest. If he hits the ball into a bunker, take

the rake to him if he didn't get it himself. We all learn by example. If you're not sure how to rake the bunker, here's a tip: smooth the entire area where you played. That means the footsteps too, not just the spot where the ball landed. It is so irritating to find yourself in a poorly raked bunker. If you want to give a good example, make an extra effort to smooth out a greenside bunker while you're waiting for the rest of the group. Courtesy like this can actually become contagious.

If you have a few seconds after hitting your shot, rake smooth a few additional footsteps when leaving the bunker. Many times players just rake the divot they made and not their footsteps. That means the bunker may be worse than before the last shot was hit!

An Important Issue

We have examined many ways to be courteous and helpful to your guest. Using them will give your guest a better experience. However, you can go overboard by trying to accommodate your guest and ultimately send the wrong message. Your guest will easily see that you are trying too hard to impress him, that your efforts are fake, and guess what? There goes the potential business situation, flying straight out-of-bounds. Double bogey.

Other Golfers

All too often we forget the players on other holes. We tend to drive right past a golfer on the adjacent fairway without stopping while he is hitting his shot, or we might be talking with a member of our group in the same situation. Other times we might be driving past a green while someone is putting. Situations arise during a round of golf when we need to exercise commonsense courtesy. The key is simple. Be aware of all those around you, and treat others the way you would like to be treated.

We All Want Exact Yardage

Television has had its effect, because many of us try to copy what the pros do. We pace off each shot to determine the exact distance to the target, as if we have the same skill level those tour professionals show us each week.

Who are these golfers who pace off the distance to the nearest yardage markers when they don't know if the ball will land within twenty yards of the pin—if they're lucky? One of our contacts in New Mexico suggests the "Star Wars" theory of club selection. He told us, "Remember the line, 'Use your feelings, Luke.' Try it sometime. You may be surprised at how good a distance judge you are and how much time you'll save during a round."

It is an important part of etiquette, and also speeds up play, to help your guest with yardage markers. Most courses have the distance to the middle or the front of the green indicated on the top of sprinkler heads. So when you are near your guest's ball, find the yardage marker quickly to determine the distance to the green.

How about a really bad lie in the fairway? What happens if your ball comes to rest in a divot? The USGA rules state that you are not allowed to move the ball from a divot. (Rule 13.1. Ball Played As It Lies.) BusinessLinks again would recommend that you follow the USGA rules. However, if the round is just for fun and if you and your guest are really struggling through the round, suggest that on the back nine everyone plays by winter rules. But establish the rules and play by them.

What about those buckets of sand on the golf cart? They are not there for the beach. Replace divots any time you can. This is another course management must. Certain courses request that you replace the divot you created with the actual tuft of grass that was cut out from the stroke you made. Courses have different types of grass, and the tuft of grass will not always grow back. Some courses ask that you replace the divot with a sand-and-seed mix supplied for you on your golf cart. On those courses, leave the divot where it landed. It is important to learn the rules for the course you are playing. The starter and course rangers are familiar with course policy, so if you aren't sure, ask what the preference is.

Replace or fill the divot for your guest if it is obvious he doesn't know the policy. This is another show-by-example situation. Have that scoop of replacement sand ready for the divots. Remember, it's courtesy golf. In fact, while you're waiting for the group in front of you, take a few seconds to fill some other divots. There's nothing wrong with getting a refill of sand at the turn. There's not a greens chairman in the world who would object to increasing the budget for more sand for the cart buckets. Suppose every golfer filled his own divots and just one more per hole all day long! Over time, that would make a difference, wouldn't it? A good goal in personal course maintenance is to return the cart at the end of the round with an empty bucket on your side of the cart.

Giving Advice

Playing With Jack Nicklaus Didn't Make Pat Nervous

Playing with Jack Nicklaus is an experience. He's very cautious about giving you information about what's wrong with your game. We played once at Doral in the pro-am. The other three guys in our fivesome had paid quite a lot of money to play with Nicklaus. I mean, these are men of substance, but they were so nervous that not one of them could draw the club back on the first tee in his presence. They finally said, "We'll meet you on the first green." Nicklaus and I played the first hole without them!

Nicklaus was a placekicker in high school, and so was I. He also played basketball. I guess he was pretty good. So we had a lot in common. But after five holes he said, "I guess you don't play much."

I said, "What do you mean?"

He looked at me cautiously and replied, "You don't know how to line up."

So he showed me how to line up. Not a bad guy to learn from, huh?

One important point is worth repeating. We mentioned this earlier in our discussion about differentials in handicaps. It is

generally a good idea not to give advice about your partner's game
unless he is substantially less skilled than you are, and only if he
asks for help. Be very careful about giving specific advice. In fact,
BusinessLinks suggests that if your guest is a poor golfer and he
asks for help, tell him to keep his head down and you will watch
the ball. That's pretty harmless advice. Unless you are a teaching
professional, you may be getting yourself in more trouble by
giving the wrong advice. You might also say, "I really can't tell
what you are doing wrong; have you thought about asking the
local pro?"

From a Low-Handicapper in North Carolina

*I don't give people swing instruction or anything like that for a
very good reason. The guy may think, "Oh, I'm having a bad day,
I usually shoot eighty-five and I'm going to shoot a hundred
today, and the person I'm playing with gave me this tip, and now
I'm going to shoot one hundred and fifty. If he gives accounting
advice like he gives swinging advice, I'll end up paying double
the taxes." I don't consider myself an expert on the swing. I think
you risk getting the relationship off on the wrong foot. Am I going
to tell you how to run your business, too? If I'm asked for help, I'll
often say, "You know, this is really not my place, and I don't care
to give advice, but I'll watch for a little while." And then I just
generally leave it alone. If he asks again, then I've got to say
something. But I don't volunteer anything.*

Ready Golf

Typically, you won't play "ready golf" until you are on the course
and are able to see how your guest is playing. (Ready golf: no
particular order of play; hit the ball when ready, but observe
safety.) Just because your partner has a higher handicap doesn't
mean that he plays slowly or doesn't know the rules. But if you
find that a hole opens in front of you and a group waiting to hit
is behind you, then be sure to enlist ready golf. Taking command

of course management and keeping up with the group in front of you shows your guest that you understand the etiquette of the game. That translates to credibility. One of the easiest ways to speed up your group is to hire a runner or a caddie, if the club offers that service. Go back to the earlier comments on caddies to review some of the benefits of having some experienced help on your side.

16

On the Green

More opportunities to show BusinessLinks skills occur on the green than any other place on the course. It is important to know the rules. Another essential is to know proper etiquette on the green. Let's focus on your partner and the different situations that take place. Of all the nuances to learn about golf, this is one area where the manners, or lack thereof, show up.

Ball Marks and Lies

The first thing you should *always* do when first stepping on the green is repair any obvious ball marks that you see. Repair your own, of course, but if your ball mark is close to your playing partner's and you get there first, fix that one too. Be sure you have the proper tool to fix ball marks. A ball mark will heal within twenty-four hours if repaired immediately. However, a ball mark left unattended will take several days to heal. A good example shows your guest a professional approach to the game. If we all thought about leaving the course in better shape than when we got to the first tee, we would all repair ball marks, fix divots, and rake bunkers. Test yourself the next time you are playing alone. How many times do you repair a ball mark or rake a bunker when no other golfer is in sight? The answer should be the same as if you were under the spotlight of the eighteenth hole with a crowd at the member-guest tournament.

Did you know that you can repair any ball marks in the path of your putt, but not spike marks? Walk carefully and check out the new soft-spike shoes. You can replace your current steel spikes with the new nonmetal spikes for only a few dollars. Most courses now require nonmetal spikes.

Did you know that there is a correct way to fix a ball mark? Take your ball mark tool and stick it straight down into the "injury." Twist the tool around. Pull it out and stick it on the outside of the ball mark at an angle into the center and carefully lift up the grass directly around the ball mark; do that completely around the mark. When finished, take your putter and tap down the earth so that it is even with the rest of the green. Then fix another one. Maybe a third, too.

Putting Courtesy

As you walk around the green, take care not to step in anyone's line. The ball farthest from the cup putts first. In many cases, someone may have to hold the pin in the cup for the person putting to see it. Offer to hold the flag even if your playing partner is fairly close to the hole. Those of us with over-forty eyesight will appreciate it.

Do you know why professional caddies hold the flag in the cup at an angle? They want to make sure that the flag is out of its holder so they don't make the mistake of getting it stuck when trying to remove it after the player has putted. If the ball hits the flagstick, there is a two-stroke penalty!

When holding the flagstick, be sure the flag is held against the pole so it doesn't flutter during someone's putt. Pull the flagstick out of its holder (not the cup). Stand so that your shadow does not fall in front of the hole. When laying the flag down, be sure that it is pointing at the hole and at least four or five yards from the hole. The reason to carefully place the flag pointing at the hole is that it helps "hide" the flagpole, and then it does not look like a backstop for the ball when someone is putting.

Be sure to give the putt to your playing partner if his putt is within the leather of your putter (typically one to two feet), assuming you agreed to this on the first tee. If he makes a good putt, acknowledge it with enthusiastic praise. No golfer ever tires of hearing "That's good," "Great putt," or "Nice shot." It's just human nature. It seems every club inevitably has an old grouch, always frowning and unpleasant. If you happen to be paired with that individual, watch his expression when you toss a compliment his way!

Be Ready to Putt When It's Your Turn

Don't spend a lot of time determining the direction of your putt when it's your turn. Line it up beforehand. Some golfers dream they are "on tour" all day long, looking at every angle of their putts and then, after what seems like an eternity, miss by a wide margin. Be still and quiet and do not stand directly behind or in front of your playing partner when he putts. Remember, the putting green is the only place where all parties (regardless of handicaps) are often on even ground. It can be the place where a less-skilled golfer makes his only recovery from the rest of his play. So be courteous. You know, every golfer can improve his stroke at home or the office with one of those silly contraptions that spits the ball back at you. A few minutes a week will work wonders on technique and confidence.

When leaving the green, make the effort to replace the flagstick. Can you count how many times you replace the flagstick during a round? Be the caddie and see to it that you replace it most of the time. Typically, the first person to putt out is responsible for replacing the flag. It is customary to wait for everyone to putt out before leaving the green; it's also just plain rude to be on the way to the cart, or on the next tee, when your group is still finishing the hole.

Many times your playing partner will approach the green with several clubs. He may have had to hit out of the sand or chip it from the side of the green. Invariably, from time to time someone will forget his club on the side of the green. Make it your business to pick it up as you leave if it's close to you.

Here's an equipment tip: every golfer should have labels on his clubs. A nominal fee is generally charged, but it is peanuts compared to the cost of a single lost golf club.

17

As a Caddie Would

Typically, the person with the lowest score on the last hole tees off first on the next hole. We know that not everyone knows or understands the rules and etiquette of golf, but, if your playing partner wants to hit first, even if he lost the last hole, let him hit it. Always stand away from the person who is hitting a shot. Don't stand directly behind him or directly behind the ball. The best place to stand is to the side, that's in front of the person as he is standing when hitting his tee shot, *not* in front of the ball! Wait until he has completely finished hitting before you move in to hit your shot. He may wait until the ball comes to rest before he gives up the box, and that's O.K. You should be watching his ball anyway. But have your ball and tee ready, and be finished with your homework on whether this is a par 4 or par 5, where to hit it, and so forth.

Keep Up With the Group in Front of You, but Don't Rush or Be Rushed

Another point should be made here. We have talked about the speed of play and that the goal is to play eighteen holes in less than three hours and forty-five minutes. Some golfers rush through the game; it makes it very difficult for everyone else to enjoy the round when someone is on the run. Keep up with the group in front of you, but don't rush or be rushed. A normal pace for a round of golf is the achievable goal, and that means less than four hours.

The key to playing golf within a reasonable period means not wasting time by:

125

1. Checking the exact yardage to the target.

2. Lining up your putt.

3. Looking for lost balls.

4. Making the turn.

5. Keeping score three or four holes at a time—get the scores on each hole.

Mulligan

- Set the format for play before you get to the first tee.

- You are obligated to follow the rules of golf, so know them well.

- If your guest has a higher handicap than you do, let him tee off first.

- Keep up the pace of play, even when balls are hit out-of-bounds, and when it's time to "pick up" and go to the next hole.

- Mark your ball.

- Fix your ball mark and any others you see.

- Start lining up your putt immediately; don't wait until it's your turn.

- Don't step in another player's line.

- If you are closest to the pin, ask if anyone would like you to hold the flag.

- If holding the flag, be sure your shadow does not cross the hole, and hold the flag still.

- If you hole out first, be first to grab the flag to replace it when everyone is finished.

- Leave the green immediately after the last person holes out.

- Five minutes is the maximum time for finding a lost ball.

- Nobody knows all the rules, so keep a copy of the USGA rule book in your bag.

- Find the distance to the hole quickly and hit the ball.

- Be sure to pay close attention to all the shots your guests make.

- Don't give advice to your guest on how to better hit the ball; think twice if he asks.

- Always replace your divot, and offer help to do the same for your guests.

- Don't enter a bunker before you locate the rake, and have it with you.

- "Pick up" your ball if you are out of the hole.

- If you begin to fall behind the group in front of you, play "ready golf."

- Think of yourself as a caddie when entertaining a guest in BusinessLinks.

Part V

ETIQUETTE

18

How to Gracefully Decline an Invitation

Here is a situation that comes up in BusinessLinks quite often. You receive an invitation to play in a tournament and for some reason you may wish to decline the offer. How do you do so without offending the host? It may be a situation where you just don't want to play at all, or you simply can't accept the invitation, but would like to be invited another time, and therefore don't want to be "off the list." If you just don't want to play, the best thing to do is to simply decline and tell the other party you appreciate the invitation, but just can't make it that day. Acknowledge that fact with some small talk about the rest of the foursome, or about the particular course. Perhaps even suggest another golfer. This takes the edge off the rejection, and also puts the potential host at ease in accepting your rejection. A graceful denial of an invitation goes a long way toward maintaining whatever relationship you have that generated the invitation, despite not being able to accept it.

In a situation where you have already determined that there is no way you are going to do any business with the potential host and you just want to cut it off, it may be difficult to be cordial, but the proper etiquette is still to be very graceful in rejecting the invitation; it's the same old story about burning bridges. If you can't play, or you don't want to play, don't play! It's an awful predicament to be in when your invited guest has accepted an invitation to play (and he knows he is tentative about playing, but not polite enough to decline), only to hear a last-minute cancellation from a jerk who really didn't want to play to begin

131

with, and you're left holding the bag with a threesome. At the same time, you can often get the same business mileage from being offered the invitation, if you have the skill to politely and inoffensively decline it.

Who Makes the Call?

On the other hand, let's take a situation where you are the host and need to fill the foursome with three other guests. It's always best to extend the invitation yourself, as opposed to having an assistant make the telephone call, and we recommend making the extra effort on your own, if you possibly can. In the event that you don't have time and just need to fill the foursome, a properly trained and understanding assistant, who knows how important golf is to your business dealings, can help tremendously in the development of your business relationship. Still, it might take seven or eight calls to fill your foursome.

You need to get across to somebody that, "Here's the game, I'm trying to fill the foursome. Here's the date and the time," and that you would like the guest to give you an answer as soon as possible. If you are trying to fill a foursome a month or two in advance, give the respondent a couple of days to get back to you. Then be certain to follow up, because the closer you get to the deadline, the tougher it is to fill the foursome. People plan their BusinessLinks outings weeks and months in advance, and they build the rest of their business schedules around the golf. Trust us, that's a true statement!

In a tournament situation, such as a member-guest or a team scramble, the closer the tournament date, the greater the pressure to fill the group. It also becomes apparent to the invited guest that he may be a little further down the list. It's okay to indicate that you've had a cancellation in your group and that it's a last-minute situation, and "Can you join us?" Then basic business sense takes control of the situation. Spend a few minutes describing the tournament, the golf course, the rest of the foursome, what their business background is, whether you have played with them before, whether somebody is a member at the club, if it includes lunch, dinner, or both, if you've played in the tournament previously, if the sponsors make it a first-class event. All those things can be explained to your guest in a couple of minutes.

Make the outing an event your guest wants to attend and be a part of. Even if the guest doesn't accept, you have made your point and have enhanced your personal relationship, even though you don't tee up together for that particular tournament. It's a good idea to keep track of those invitations, even to the point of having some sort of golf folder or computer file for business associates that you want to invite, or a list of those who invited you to play. The main point here is to be graceful in acknowledging the invitation, and either accepting or rejecting it based on common business sense. Cordiality is the rule. Keep in mind that if you really don't want to play with that group, don't accept the invitation. Suggest somebody else for the foursome so the group can be put together and everybody can enjoy it. A last-minute cancellation, leaving your host scrambling to fill the foursome, borders on insult.

19

The Finer Points

The Wrong Score!

1968 sticks out in my memory, too. It was my first year announcing the Masters. That's the year that Roberto DeVicenzo and Bob Goalby had the match down the stretch. Tommy Aaron put down the wrong score on DeVicenzo's scorecard and he signed it. If DeVicenzo had signed the correct score they would have had a playoff. After I had announced that there would be a playoff, the producer told me not to say it again because there might be a problem with his scorecard. I'm thinking, how do I apologize for saying that, although you never think there might be a mistake in a tournament of that magnitude. We had a microphone in the scorer's tent and I remember him saying, "I am a stupid, I am a stupid." He never blamed anyone; he was very gracious. There's no telling what would have happened to DeVicenzo's career if he had won that tournament. Goalby won a tainted championship and he's still bitter about it today.

Who Keeps Score?

If you're the driver, you may be in charge of keeping the score. Circle the holes which either you, your guest, or the other members of your group, have extra shots on, based on handicaps. Many golfers like to keep score as well as keep track of the wagers. Ask your guest if he is interested or would like to do so, then suggest that he drive as well.

134

For several reasons, you may want to keep score whenever you can. It forces you to write down everyone's name so you don't forget. That is helpful in the charity scramble or the resort game, where you may not know the other golfers. It allows your guest to focus on golf and having a good time. If you are the scorer, it is your responsibility to keep track of any adjustments that should be made on the tenth tee. Basically, put the work on yourself and let your guest relax. Remember that you can't make adjustments on the tenth tee unless you state so on the first tee. Well, you can, but it's more fun to set the competitive juices on the first tee, and it makes for better nineteenth hole discussions when the day's activities are reviewed four hours later.

The gentle jabs really fly when we are reminded that we won the front nine, but lost the back nine or played awful, and therefore lost both nines. Or, since both nines were lost, the tab should get picked up by the winners, which is often more expensive than the lost bets.

The court understands that the defendant lied about his handicap, but there are no grounds for the death penalty.

Determine the type of golf you are going to play before you get started. This would include the special rules you may establish: mulligans off the first tee; winter rules; gimmies within the leather, and others.

What Did You Say Your Score Was?

Don't assume your guest's score. Ask him what he made on the last hole. You may find that he gives himself a lower score than he actually shot. This is another tough call. The best way to deal with this situation is to review each shot with your guest on the first couple of holes. This allows him to see his real score and sets the tone for the rest of the round. If you are the scorekeeper, get the scores after each hole, particularly when you are wagering. When there are several holes to record it is easy to make an error, it takes longer, and it may inadvertently irritate your playing partners. Another tip is to ask everyone's score when they are all together, which would be on the next tee. It's much harder for someone to misstate his score in front of the group. Again, if your guest has a problem with keeping his correct score, either suggest an accountant or just don't do business with him.

Who Rides Together in the Carts?

Let's assume that we are a foursome at the course. We have electric carts, so who rides with whom? It may seem obvious, but if this is a round of BusinessLinks, then the two decision-makers should ride together. It is not like a courtroom where an adversarial relationship exists. The purpose is to advance the relationship in some manner, so it helps to ride together. But the decision has to be made before you ride off into the sunset. Otherwise, it is uncomfortable, it appears that the day was not really thought out, and two people find themselves riding with their fellow employee.

Incidentally, when a friendly wager is made on the first tee, some golfers like to ride with the playing partner. This is particularly true with the better golfers and when the stakes are higher, because they do much strategizing on the course, and it is helpful if your partner is at your side. In a BusinessLinks game, where the stakes are at most bragging rights and maybe $20 or $50, it is still good for the decision-makers to ride together, even if they are not playing partners. All the little idiosyncrasies of golfers come out regardless of the wager, so for the overall relationship it is better to ride with the person who is key to the business decision that will ultimately be made.

Speed of Play Tip

Scores should be recorded at the next tee, not on the green, nor in the cart next to the green just finished. This courtesy may seem obvious, but watch how many times play is delayed because the scorer is diligently recording the event but holding up play. Move on to the next tee before the pencil is picked up.

BusinessLinks promotes the principle of "golf by the rules." That's why a 30-plus handicapper and a tour player can easily play a round of golf together and have the time of their lives. Since golf brings out our true character, we shouldn't bend the rules. The message sent to your group can negatively affect the potential relationship if the rules are not followed. There are many golfers who do cheat, and it's those individuals of whom you must be wary, both on and off the course. If the ball lands in a divot, play it from the divot. If your ball is behind a tree, play it where it lands. Some people believe it is okay to help out the guest, moving it so that he has a better chance to score. But the message sent to the guest is: if he helps me cheat, then he must cheat too. Play by the rules agreed to on the first tee. In most games, business golf or simply a casual round with friends, following the rules should be the game plan.

Is There Rest for the Weary at Halftime?

Making the turn on some courses can take more time than you expect. Most courses have a snack bar with food and drinks available between the ninth and tenth holes. As a BusinessLinks player, check to see what your guest wants (hot dog, beverage, cigar, etc.) on the fairway of the eighth hole (some courses have a call box on the ninth tee). Make the turn as fast as you can in order to keep up with the party in front of you. A normal pace of play allows about five minutes for the halftime show. If the group behind you begins to approach the turn and your group is delayed, then you need to move on. If your group has been holding up the group behind, this is also a good time to offer them the chance to play through.

What's the Ruling on This? A Frustrated Resort Professional Confides

I'm amazed at how many people don't know the rules. They put clubs on the ground in the bunkers; they don't know when they can get a free drop and when they don't get a drop, but it doesn't matter, because they don't know where to drop it anyway! They don't know about penalties and the rub of the green, or the difference between lateral hazards and out of bounds. They don't know the difference between red stakes and yellow stakes. They think "No Hunt" is an instruction to "leave your rifle at home."

Should You Play and Smoke?

For most folks, smoking is taboo. Make sure before you light a cigar or cigarette that you will not offend anyone in the group. If you have carefully planned the round, there is no choice if your guest doesn't care for smoking.

Additionally, if someone in the other cart complains about smoking, don't smoke. The fact that you're not in the same cart with the nonsmokers doesn't mean their noses don't work. Another smoking tip—throw the butts in the trash, not the bunker. Cigars, when finished, offer good nutrients to the soil. Make sure they're out and toss them into dense bushes, but pull the label off first, and dispose of it properly. By the way, cigarette filters are not biodegradable like natural tobacco in a cigar.

The Famous Jessie and Martin: Alcohol and BusinessLinks

We know of a turn stand that pours unusually strong drinks, and the club charges appropriately. The attendants are Jessie and Martin, and it's not uncommon for some unknowing guests to feel no pain if they are not properly coached. The terminology used is that sometimes the group gets Jessitized or Martinized, and we're not talking about dry-cleaning.

Another Commonsense Tale, Anonymous for Obvious Reasons

I'll never forget the time I invited a guest and we started drinking on the first hole. By the ninth hole we were on our third drink. From what I remember we were laughing, telling wild tales, and generally having a great time. As we finished the round we had consumed a few beers and several hard drinks. My guest was definitely feeling it, and when we got to the bar after the round I had him eating out of my hand. He was getting loud and a little obnoxious and started bragging about his business and other things I won't mention. I was sure I had him committed. Mind you, this was the first time that I had been with this individual on a social basis. A couple of days later I called him to make an appointment to finalize the deal. He took my call but his tone was completely different. He sounded almost cold and to the point. When I asked him about what we had discussed after golf that day, he said he didn't remember and that he wasn't interested. I couldn't believe it. The only thing I can figure out was that he was embarrassed about the way he acted that day. I never had him as a guest again and was unable to do any business with his company.

Some courses have a beverage cart that drives around the course throughout your round. Based on the new laws against drinking and driving and common courtesy, don't encourage alcohol consumption (if you are playing BusinessLinks, be extra careful that you don't drink too much). Not only will it impair your judgment; it can certainly affect the entire experience in a negative fashion. Better to play it safe.

How Do You Deal With a Guest Who Cheats?

This question is one of the most frequently asked. It's a tough call. On the one hand, you are trying to arrange some sort of business with this person; on the other hand, you know that he's cheating. If your guest cheats, do you really want to do business with him? The true spirit of the game is simple: play by the rules. Our suggestion on dealing with a guest who cheats is to explain to him that you play by the rules that were established on the first tee. If your guest has a hard time with the fact that the group agreed on the rules, then you can bet that he may cheat in business as well. You will find that most golfers will respect you for playing by the rules and enforcing them with your guests.

Cheat in Golf, Cheat in Business?

One of our interviews with a 20-handicap stockbroker yielded the following story.

Not too long ago I had the opportunity to play with someone whom I thought was going to be a wonderful new business relationship. On about the fourteenth hole I had had enough. It was quite obvious that this guy was satisfied with his existing relationship, and I had a 10 percent chance of "getting the order." He was a pompous jerk, and I did everything I could not to talk to him. On the next hole he really showed me his colors. He hit a slice deep into the woods. He went out after it and you could hear him hacking away. A few minutes later you see this ball land about three feet from the pin—but it's yellow! That's what is great about golf; it helps you understand personalities. If the guy is going to go roaring in the woods after he hits a white ball and come out with a yellow ball and then say he's got a bogey—holy cow! What's he going to do in a business setting?

Here is a tip about penalty strokes; it is an easy way to remember the rules. If a free drop is allowed, it is always one club length. If there is a penalty stroke involved, you may drop within two club lengths. Think of it as paying for the cost of the extra club length with an additional stroke.

20

Cart Etiquette and General Safety

Driving a cart ought to be an innocent enough task. Amazingly, serious accidents and mishaps occur too often as a result of inconsiderate actions. Keep in mind that if you are driving, you are the taxi driver. That way you will always be thinking about your guest's ball first.

Safety Belts? This Architect Could Have Used One

I'll never forget the day I threw my partner out of the cart. I was driving on the left side of the fairway at full speed (which isn't very fast, as you know) and we were looking for my ball, which was somewhere in the rough. My playing partner was a man of about fifty, and he was leaning forward in his seat to get a cigarette. I wasn't paying attention, and as we were zipping down the fairway I noticed my ball to the left. Immediately, I turned hard to the left and heard a loud moan coming from my partner, who was now sprawled out on the fairway. I've never felt so embarrassed in all my life. Fortunately, he did not break or sprain anything, but he sure let me have it when he got back in. I noticed that he hung on to the armrest for the rest of the round. This man was president of a large company, they were thinking of using our firm to design their building, and I was following up on a very fruitful initial meeting the month before our game. This all happened on the first hole, and the rest of the day was tense, to say the least. Forget about business, I was glad he didn't sue me!

Follow the Cart Rules and You
Won't Embarrass Yourself

Golf cart etiquette may seem simple, but there are many things to consider. First, most carts have places for drinks. Golf carts are made to drive throughout the course. They drive well on the cart paths, the fairways, the rough, in the woods, just about anywhere. But one thing is certain—they have the suspension of a tank without seat belts! Quick turns and any undulation on the ground, no matter how small, and your partner's drink is all over his shoes. Be careful when chauffeuring your guest around. Commonsense tip: if the beverage cart has tops for the cups, use them.

Who Drives the Cart?

We surveyed many golfers on the question of who drives the cart. One of our respondents, a retired psychology professor, told us: "I always let my guest drive the cart. I like for him to be in control and it gives me an opportunity to see how much he knows about golf etiquette."

We heard a different angle from a 6-handicap dentist who plays twice weekly and considers himself a very avid golfer: "It's a good idea to have the better golfer drive the cart, if there is a substantial difference in skill level. The higher-handicap player will have more 'stops' to make, so the better player can be in control of the cart, help with finding golf balls, and so forth." We have all heard of the cart that went into the pond. How? One person was addressing his ball while the other was near the pond getting ready to hit his shot. The golfer near the pond parked the cart on the slope and forgot to engage the brake properly, so the unattended cart simply rolled in. It may seem funny, but it was really very serious, very dangerous, and very costly. By the way, how is your personal umbrella insurance coverage?

More on Mickey Mantle From Pat

I played a lot of golf with Mickey Mantle. He was about a 5 or 6 handicap in his good days. He always putted with a golf ball with baseball laces painted on it. He was not a very good putter, but he

*could hit the ball a mile. He was a good driver of the golf ball, but
not of the golf cart. He could drive a ball anywhere, but he was
the worst cart driver I ever knew. Cart paths meant nothing to
him; he just drove. He would drive the cart at breakneck speed,
as fast as it would go, no matter how many curves were on the
path. Yet somehow he never had an accident.*

You Drive

When driving to the next tee after putting out, be sure to
approach carefully so as not to disturb the player teeing off.

This is an area where many golfers don't show proper consideration. The best approach is to think of the ride to the next
tee as a courtesy ride—be courteous to all the golfers you come
into contact with.

Here is an interesting aside from an automobile dealer who
claims at least three business golf rounds monthly, and who
always lets his guest drive the cart:

*Even if it's my club, my guest drives. It gives me an opportunity to
look at him a little bit. I can watch him, the way he handles the
golf cart, if he runs up too close to the green. Those are just a
lot of things that I have picked up over the years observing
somebody for four hours driving a golf cart. It might not make a
lot of sense to everybody, but it's helped me assess many business relationships.*

On many courses we are required to drive only on the cart path.
Proper etiquette says always take the cart to the closest point near
your guest's ball. If your ball is located farther away than his,
then leave the cart, take a few clubs in your hand, and ask your
guest to meet you further down the path. This speeds up play
and also shows consideration to your guest.

The Perils of Golf

Nobody really thinks of golf as a dangerous sport. Quite the con-
trary, most people would view golf as a relaxing, slow, and gentle

game. Why not? You can play it your entire life. Seems sort of harmless. Let's talk about the dangers of golf.

Literally speaking, a golf ball, when hit by any one of your clubs, travels at a velocity of nearly 250 feet per second in the initial explosion period (the first thirty yards). The ball has a weight of 1.62 ounces and a diameter of 1.68 inches. In order for the ball to travel at such speeds and be a specified weight it must also be very hard. So the ball becomes a lethal projectile that has maimed, crippled, and even killed its unintended victims.

Most golfers do not consider that their playing partner, much like himself (no matter what handicap), has control problems with virtually every shot he hits. If you are standing in front or to the side of the person who is hitting the ball, there is always a chance of becoming the unintended target.

It's Not Always the Fault of the Person Who Hits the Ball

Being hit by a golf ball is not our idea of a pleasant experience. What about the person who hit the shot? Safety is a two-way street. Not only must you watch out for anyone in front of you before you hit, you must also be aware of those around you at all times. Many courses have tight fairways that are next to one another, with only a few trees dividing them, thus placing nearby golfers in a tenuous position when an errant shot finds its way to the adjacent hole.

If you notice your shot traveling anywhere in the direction of golfers you are obligated to yell loudly, "Fore!" Imagine if you hit a poor shot that struck another golfer and you didn't have the presence of mind to yell, "Fore!" Imagine that the person you hit was six feet, ten inches tall, and weighed three hundred pounds. Do you think he might be a little angry?

We have all, at one time or another (some all the time), hit our shot and moved down the hole before the next person has hit his ball. How many times have you stood behind a tree waiting for the person behind you to hit? It's not always the fault of the person who hits the ball if he hits the person in front of him. Again, we are caught sitting on that double-edged wedge: we need to keep up the pace of play, but we need to wait for the next person to hit.

I thought all the golf carts had anti-lock brakes.

I Was Hit in the Head and Went Down Like a Rock!

A sad report from a once very happy, but now injured, avid golfer.

Several years ago I was playing with three other fellows on a drizzly afternoon. I was careful about watching each player hit so a ball didn't hit me. On the back nine, par 5, we had all hit our drives and they were all somewhat close to each other. This particular hole was next to the driving range. After we hit our second shots, and as I was putting my club in my bag, one of the younger fellows decided to hit a range ball that had found its way onto the course back to the range. I had no idea he was about to hit it, and was he very close, and aimed in my direction. Suddenly, I heard him strike the ball, and the next thing I remember was waking up in the hospital. He hit the ball and did not warn me, and the ball hit the side of my head just below the temple. They told me that I went down like a rock and blood was everywhere. The ball had broken the bones around my cheek and jaw. I was lucky to have survived. I spent six weeks in intensive care and continue to have plastic surgery to repair my face. It has been three years since I have picked up a club, and needless to say I will probably never play the game like I used to. If I could recommend anything to all golfers: Think before you hit and don't hit a ball anywhere near the direction of someone else. You may change your life and someone else's forever.

Mother Nature

There are other dangerous possibilities on the golf course. The most deadly is lightning. Most people are unaware of its unpredictable nature. Golfers have been hit by lightning they thought was still four miles away. Fortunately, there is new and improved technology that warns the golf shop how far from the course a lightning storm is likely to be. This allows management to sound the alarm, requiring golfers to get off the course. But not all courses have this technology. Some of the latest technology is automatic, so the pro doesn't have the choice of delaying the decision to halt play. It would be just your luck that a severe storm cloud approached just as you moved to the seventeenth tee during the round of your life.

Remember the preacher in the movie *Caddyshack?* He was playing in the rain with Carl, missed a putt, yelled something foul, and raised his club in the air, only to get struck to the ground by lightning. Death by lightning. Carl looked to see if anyone saw the mishap, and upon further review, continued on with the round. Nice guy.

Back to the real world. When the siren blares, you can continue and hopefully beat the storm before it strikes, or you can play it safe, leave immediately, and live to play another day. If you happen to be one with the writers we'll certainly meet you in the clubhouse, no questions asked. We like life. If you have invited a guest to play, it's up to you to take appropriate precautions. Of course, the point is to be cautious at all times. Your mother said not to play with matches, too.

Certain times of the year can be dangerous due to the heat and humidity. If you are not used to very high temperatures and high humidity, then don't play during the heat of the day, or be sure to take lots of water and something to cover your head. Golf is not a sport that requires the same amount of physical endurance that some other sports do. Therefore, what may seem like a nonthreatening afternoon of fun in the sun may turn out to be a sunstroke or worse, especially if you are drinking alcoholic beverages. It's not a bad idea to have a fresh cup of ice cold water for your group at the first tee, then constantly replenish it through the day. One other very important point: use sunscreen all the time, and teach young golfers to do the same. The long-term effect of not doing so helps keep the American Cancer Society in business. Get in the habit of protecting yourself, your skin, and teaching others, by example, to do the same. Younger golfers who look up to us as role models are especially vulnerable to bad habits, so let's all do our part in setting a good example.

Some golf courses are more dangerous than others with regards to the natural elements. In sunny Florida, for example, there are courses that harbor large alligators. Many of these same courses have a variety of poisonous snakes and spiders. Everyone needs to take care before walking into the out-of-bounds areas, lakes, ponds, and woods. If there is a sign that says No Hunt, you should not hunt for your golf ball in that area. The purpose is twofold: it may be environmentally sensitive and, as such, part of the natural beauty; or there may be dangerous varmints in them thar' woods.

The Club Throwers

It may seem strange to have to mention the "whirly bird," but experience has proven again that throwing your clubs is not only stupid, but dangerous. Hot-tempered individuals who have hurled a club or two into the air soon find out that clubs are not meant to fly. In fact, they are incredibly dangerous and have wounded many unintended victims. How do you deal with a guest who throws his clubs? It's easy: Tell him that if the marshal sees him throwing a club, your membership may be jeopardized. Or, you can explain that you once learned about a person who wrapped his club around a tree, it broke off, and the shaft went firmly into his neck. True story!

I Heard This Whirlybird Sound

We know of another rather humorous story about an excellent amateur player. On the eighteenth hole, following a less than satisfying round, he heaved the entire golf bag into the nearby pond, obviously somewhat disgusted. In the grille room later, he realized that his expensive watch was in the bag, so he solicited the help of the cart attendant to retrieve it from eight feet of murky water. They found it; he took out the watch, and then immediately threw the bag back in the water.

Basil Rathbone, and a Game With Pat at Pebble

I was at Pebble Beach one time when Basil Rathbone, the actor who played Sherlock Holmes, was playing in the Pro-Am, the Crosby Clambake. He hit a ball in the water at seventeen. He had been playing badly, so he went up on the rock at the eighteenth tee and told the caddie to bring him the golf bag. He took the clubs one by one and threw them as far as he could out into the Pacific. Then he took all the balls and threw them into the ocean. Then the bag went into the Pacific, then each shoe. Then he realized we had all this on camera. He turned and grabbed his caddie and started to throw him into the ocean. That's as good as I've ever seen.

Mulligan

- Know how to gracefully decline an invitation so that no bridge is burned.
- Be aware of other golfers around you, and practice good etiquette.
- Always look for your guest's ball and watch his shots.
- Always leave the course in better shape than when you arrived.
- If you and your guest's shots are relatively close to each other, let your guest hit first.

- Be courteous at all times, but don't go overboard.
- Watch out for other golfers on the course.
- Alcohol should be used in moderation on the course.
- Drive the cart carefully and always keep safety in mind.
- Follow the course rules in all instances.
- Remember that your personality is showing.
- Drink plenty of water.
- Use sunscreen and common sense.

Part VI

THE NINETEENTH HOLE

21

Special Presentation

A quality gift is a classy way to say thank you, and can go a long way in developing a good relationship. One of the nicest gifts you can give is a distinctive divot tool or a shirt with your company logo on it. If you don't have a company logoed shirt, purchase a shirt with the logo of the golf course you just played. The presentation of the gift should be casual and quick: "John, I make it a practice to present my guests with a small token of thanks the first time we play together." A short and sweet presentation is the object, and done properly and simply, reflects a touch of class.

Another gift idea is a picture of your foursome with the names, date, and location where you played. The picture can be placed in a scanner and manipulated to fit into a special bag tag with the name of your company on the back, or it can be made into a screen-saver. You can accomplish this easily with a digital camera. We know a few friends who carry a small camera and always take a photo of the group. What a good way to chronicle your golf memories.

If not everyone is a guest, be cognizant of how you present your gift. You don't want to embarrass either your guest or the others in the group. Make the presentation private, perhaps at the car when the clubs are being dropped off.

Sammy Davis Jr., One of Pat's Favorite Memories

Sammy Davis Jr. was the most generous personal host I've known. When he was involved with the Greater Hartford Open, he would go into the pro shop and buy four or five sets of the finest clubs they had. He would buy a total wardrobe and give it to people. Obviously he had the means to do it, and not everybody does. I watched him give away six sets of golf clubs at one tournament to guys who needed them, not just some other celebrity player.

Some golfers prefer to offer a gift prior to starting the round, while others like to wait until the nineteenth hole or the club-house. Over the years, our experience has shown that the best time for a gift is at the nineteenth hole. Sometimes your guest may have a poor round and may feel disappointed at his performance. A gift at the nineteenth hole has a way of turning disappointment into triumph. At the same time, if you end up with a bad experience, for whatever reason, maybe the cost of that shirt ought to be spent on yourself.

There are all kinds of items you can present to help a guest cherish the moment. The idea is to provide a reminder of the round you and your guest just played. Logoed golf balls tend to be used in the next round your guest plays and usually find their way into a hazard. Therefore, a gift that lasts is preferable. We like the shirt suggestion because we have yet to see a shirt in the eighth hole hazard. Nice-looking divot tools with logos are also lasting gifts.

Golfers—and company policy—reflect different philosophies regarding whether a gift should be presented. Some golfers believe that gifts make a guest uncomfortable. Your guest might feel obligated to return the favor or feel he or she is now indebted to you. However, experience has shown that the presentation of a gift has gone over very well and has not made the guest uncomfortable. It is a gesture of appreciation, so it's a judgment call on your part. Just use common sense.

Here's a key tip on gifts. If they are given with sincerity, they will be graciously accepted, and appreciated. If they are poor quality, it doesn't matter what they cost, the gift will reflect poorly on you and the company you represent. An $80 sterling divot repair tool, or a $15 stainless tool, lasts far beyond the sleeve of golf balls, and perhaps longer than the $75 shirt. Think about what you are trying to accomplish, then go about it in a classy way.

Here's a thought for those executives worried about the company stock of new golf balls being depleted by their increasing number of golfing employees. The concern is that the advertising budget is too high already, and now golf balls are being supplied to all our employees who are new to the game, and the balls are ending up in lakes! One of our friends, a CPA who now runs a public company in the environmental waste business, told us his employees are not allowed to play with their company golf balls, but they can give away as many as they want. Sort of puts the marketing into perspective, doesn't it?

22
Follow-Up

It seems that the nineteenth hole is where most business is won or lost. If it is lost, the reason is typically poor planning and little, if any, follow-up. Earlier in this book we discussed the critical aspect of planning the outing. One objective of BusinessLinks is to plan in advance for various outcomes.

Have a Carefully Planned Follow-Up Procedure for Every Round

(BusinessLinks Tenth Commandment)

1. Determine three different outcomes you would like to see happen from best to worst and achieve at least one of them at the nineteenth hole. (e.g., ask if you have any relationship possibility; get the introduction to the decision-maker; simply say thank you for the existing relationship; obtain a referral).

2. Get an agreement to have the next meeting in the office, preferably not your own.

3. Send a thank you letter or note after the round.

4. Update your files, fill out the company form that shows how you used that corporate dollar, and tickle the calendar for your next follow-up.

Ultimately you may find that the nineteenth hole is just a time for relaxation and reflection on the past four hours you just spent with your guest. Naturally, you have to settle all the wagers, give each other a jab or two about the game, exchange business cards, or at least determine if there may be another game in the offing. Let the conversation "weave its web" of mystical bonding powers, which are somewhat exclusive to this sport. Our tennis and fishing friends may argue a bit on this point, but we know better, right? Develop the rapport and personal relationship destined to last for years to come. Focus on the day's events and follow the discussion in whatever direction makes sense. Our experience is that the time following the round is one of simple camaraderie, not the time to press an issue of business, unless it developed on the course and you agreed to discuss it further after the round. Even then, be aware that it can ruin the outing if the stage is not properly set. For this reason, we like to make the appointment to discuss business at another time when it is strictly a business setting.

The bottom line is simple. If you have developed a genuine bond, you know very well that some business, "if at all possible," will follow. Enjoy your new friendship and relax. If you are confident that you have a genuine friendship, then your playing partner will happily take your call another time. If your guest can't or doesn't want to do business with you, don't give up. Ask for referrals. Don't be obnoxious; consider the opportunity. This BusinessLinks day may only be the first step of a long-term relationship. Whatever approach you use, be sincere, and the odds are in your favor that you'll make a new friend or two. If you are uncertain, talk to your mentor and get some help on how to follow up.

After the round is over, you have a perfect opportunity to take the next step.

You Have Earned the Right

The nineteenth hole, or clubhouse, can cement your relationship and provide you with an opportunity to accomplish your ultimate goals. You just spent four hours making certain your guest had a great time playing golf; now you both know a little about each other. You have earned the right to ask specific questions regarding business, and you can both determine if the chemistry is such that a business relationship makes sense. Where else but through golf can you have such an extended time to get to know your guest-prospect-playing partner? If you can't talk a little business by now, be satisfied that at least you made it to the course that day. In the experiences we have had, it is a rare exception that, by the end of the round, virtually all the information needed to assess the chances of success in the business relationship have not already been posted, waiting for retrieval the next time it makes sense to do so. Remember, that could be the next day or next year, but whenever it is, the opening line of the call will be about the round of golf.

Does Your Company Have a Golf Mentor?

So who is a good mentor? It could be one of the golfers in your organization who has been particularly adept at developing relationships. It could be your immediate supervisor or somebody in the marketing area. It could be a person in the company who may not play golf but may give some insight on the customer representative you just entertained. It could also be the number one person in your company who is the ultimate decision-maker and who eventually authorizes the dollars spent on business golf.

We are seeing much more acceptance in the corporate world for the line employee, not just the account executive, spending entertainment dollars. It is an absolute proven concept that in the business world, all other things being equal, relationships will win the sale. So whoever has the relationship really has the responsibility to look out for the company's interest, and that is not always the individual who is servicing the account. This is a subject that covers many bookshelves, so we won't go into it any further here.

We do believe that every person in the organization should have business cards, regardless of what their job description entails. Every employee knows at least one golfer, and as corporate golf grows, even the nongolfer can help a customer or vendor relationship. We predict much more involvement in the development of business golf relationships by the nongolfer employee, as the corporate world learns more about BusinessLinks strategies.

Learn to Track Your BusinessLinks Progress

At this point you may have spent a great deal of time planning and implementing this outing. In some cases the time is more than you would have used to plan other business meetings. So be dedicated to trying to achieve your ultimate goal, and be sure to track each event.

One method of tracking the business success of a round of golf is to keep a log which includes all the details about the relationship, information which will be needed to do the follow-up, with specific details regarding your guest and the outing. The log should include basics like the date and the course played. It should note your guest handicaps, maybe even the type of clubs and ball used, as well as club membership information. The log would also indicate the purpose of the outing and what goals you had in mind.

After the round you have several options for follow-up. What was created is nothing more complicated than a road map. Was there some inquiry during the day about another outing, or about continuing to develop the relationship began with that double-bogey-filled day at an expensive resort location? What is the logical next step to take with the business contact you just spent four or five hours with? Management can review your log and help with follow-ups. Over time you can measure to what degree your golf ventures are productive.

Let's face it, golf costs need to be justified, especially if the company is picking up the tab. Companies that use golf as a relationship tool and who are willing to pay the price should expect accountability. As golf continues to grow, we predict much more activity in this area of the corporate budgeting process. The software applications to assist in this regard are plentiful, so there are no excuses allowed when it comes to accountability.

Thank-You Letters

A thank-you letter, note, or card sent the day after the round is a great way to follow up. The card may indicate that you will call later on in the week for an appointment. You often have to play

golf more than once with a prospect in order to close a transaction. Tough duty! Need a substitute? You may develop a regular golf outing with your prospect, especially if he is a potential source of referrals. Generally, after a round of golf, your prospect is very receptive and honest in business discussions. Make the most of that.

A Low Handicapper in Texas Told Us

My philosophy is simple. If I am going to use golf as a business development tool, then I'm going to take the time to play it as well as I can. I spend a lot of time practicing. So when a business contact calls me and says, "Hey, we have a scramble scheduled and we need a good player," my chances of getting invited are enhanced. Many of these events are charity tournaments which represent occasions to give, and at the same time offer great net-working opportunities.

Other Business Development Ideas

One of the most satisfying parts of the game are the true friend-ships that a golfer develops with acquaintances and business asso-ciates. We have mentioned before that it does not matter what handicap the golfer brings to the course if the knowledge of how to communicate with others is in your bag when the first tee is in sight. But let's share some real-life stories about camaraderie around the game, which will give the reader some ideas on how to make the most of business relationships without even teeing up.

There are professional tournaments every week in major cities throughout the country, and we can spend all of a weekend in front of the big screen watching golf skills exhibited in envi-able fashion by the greatest names in the game. There are oppor-tunities to learn the game by watching the pros on television, but why not get a group together and actually make a trip to one of the events? Expense is certainly a factor, but if a tournament is in the area, the cost consists of, in most cases, $8 to $12 per person. All of the tournaments have package deals, and they really are bargains if properly used. The point here is to make use of the time to get to know your business associates, whether a fellow employee, a prospect, or an existing relationship, by spending some time on the course watching others who can hit it a little better than the rest of us.

Our experience shows that once the group has reached its destination, whether it is a professional tournament, a close-by but still out-of-town pro-am, or just an outing of a foursome at the closest resort, the whole mood of the group changes. There is always a little excitement about seeing a new course, or one of the many new stars out there on tour, and it is always relaxing to just plain get away from it all. It is normal for a guest to be the first to offer to buy the refreshments while the group is walking from hole to hole. Here you are in a wonderful environment, casually strolling on a beautiful golf resort, sipping a cold beer, watching the professionals earn their living, being entertained by (at times) some of the funniest athletes, so is anything more appropriate to create an aura of camaraderie than this? Over the next two or three hours, do you think it is possible to tell that person that your relationship is important to you and your company, that it is appreciated, and that you are glad to have the time to spend in this casual setting, and, by the way, I sure would like to get in the running for that next opportunity being considered by your CEO? Whatever it is you buy or sell, golf can create the unique setting to promote the relationship.

Mulligan

- Make your special presentation after the round, and do it with subtlety.

- Whatever gift you present, make it first class.

- Follow-up is one of the keys to making BusinessLinks profitable.

- Impress your guest with your communication skills as well as your shot-making skills.

Part VII

TOURNAMENTS

23

Hooked on Golf

Pat was recently asked about the effect television had on the average golfer, and he told the reporter:

I did not think as many golfers would watch television as the statistics show. I was wrong. The Golf Channel has been a startling success. It's strange how many different aspects there are to golf that we can get wrapped up in. We see golfers who get charged up about the different clubs the professionals play with and they end up constantly changing their own equipment. I have a pretty big collection I've picked up over the years. Others are obsessed with tinkering with their swings all the time. Some people make it a life's study to learn about the many great golf courses of the world and they play several each year, eventually realizing it will never end. We are all so influenced by the media, by the personalities we watch and the stories told. There are golfers who are into their own competitions and their own score. There are others who follow the professionals on all the tours around the world in great detail. It is an infatuating game. There are a myriad of ways to be an avid golfer.

Attending golf events is a regular part of life for BusinessLinksers. There is a group in Tampa that has made an annual event out of going to Augusta in April for the Masters, with different guests each year, all of whom have some business relationship that undoubtedly is enhanced by the experience. With the very limited ticket availability at Augusta, the venue moves to Bay Hill, in

165

Orlando, Florida, or the Tournament Players Championship, in Jacksonville, or the Suncoast Seniors, at TPC Tampa Bay. It is a routine part of BusinessLinks to attend professional events, and the enjoyment of getting to know the business associate creates a lasting image that transcends the event itself and makes for a better business relationship throughout the year. It works. Try it. You can spend as much as you care to entertain friends and customers. You can get by with minimal amounts, or you can go bananas and rent homes at the sites, furnish dinners, airfares, or whatever it takes to accomplish the objective set up in advance.

From Announcing to Playing the Game

I'll tell you how golf can get a hold on us. When the season was over for the CBS announcers we all went to North Carolina to play golf. It was a great experience, just the announcers, no pros. It's funny, when our work was over we chose to go out and play the game we talked about. In my experience, it's the only sport where you covered it and became enamored with it and then tried to play it and enjoyed playing what you talked about. I don't know of any football announcers who go out and play touch football or baseball announcers who get together for softball.

It's amazing how you can watch those perfect swings over and over. You know what is supposed to happen just from watching it. You know what you are supposed to do but you just can't do it.

Another Successful Executive Woman Golfer

As a senior officer in my company, I am often asked to mentor younger associates. When asked how to better relate to clients, advance business development endeavors, or network within my organization, I always recommend playing golf. I expect to see more and more companies encouraging and subsidizing its employees' development of golf skills. Way to go, BusinessLinks!

Like any event you wish to attend, plan in advance. There are a number of considerations to be accounted for. Professional events have practice rounds prior to the actual tournament. These are in the beginning of the week and are less crowded. The practice rounds present an opportunity to watch the players hit multiple shots from the same spot, particularly around the green (more than two shots from the fairway is discouraged, but watching the skills of the professionals around the green make the outing well worth the effort). While the practice rounds are loose and more informal than the actual event, the rules of etiquette still apply.

The tickets for the practice rounds are lower-priced than tournament days, so purchase several and entertain more than one guest at a time. Corporate-sponsored tickets are often given away, thinking the same advantage is gained with clients or prospects, as would be the case if the guest was personally escorted to the event. Remember, golf is a personal experience, and in order to make the most of it for business development purposes one must not only attend, but extra steps should be taken to develop a personal relationship with those who are invited.

There are certain tournaments where people from all over the world gather. One is the Masters in Augusta. In many enthusiasts' minds, the Masters is considered the most prestigious tournament in the world. Businesses from around the world make arrangements years in advance and even make travel arrangements for their guest clients. Tens of thousands of dollars are spent by single companies as part of their corporate business development plan, with the best clients and top prospects invited with all costs paid. The Who's Who of golf attend the Masters every year, and in most cases obtaining tickets is impossible, especially during the actual event itself. Members and families who have owned tickets for generations control the show. This is one event you have to plan for months, if not years, in advance. If you know a special person who likes golf, one of the finest compliments you can provide is to arrange a trip to the Masters.

Pat Announced Jack's Last Masters Victory

The most memorable experience in golf was broadcasting the Masters, being at the eighteenth hole, particularly in 1986, when Jack Nicklaus won with his son caddying. Nobody gave him a chance to win the tournament at the age of forty-six. He just played so well, particularly on the back nine. I'll always remember the noise coming from "Amen Corner" and the atmosphere of him winning. You could hear the roars coming from the back nine. After you've been at Augusta for awhile you can tell by the crowd roars. There are eagle roars and birdie roars, and you know which hole it's coming from after you get used to it. You know what's going on without even seeing a scoreboard.

Seeing him walk up to the eighteenth hole—the tremendous ovation he received, the throng that followed him, the fact that his son was carrying his bag—it's probably the most emotional I've ever been in broadcasting. I'm glad I didn't have to say anything because the sound and the scene carried itself. I don't think I could have said anything if I had to. It was just overwhelming.

Next to that was being at the eighteenth hole in 1975. Again Nicklaus was involved, but both Johnny Miller and Tom Weiskopf had putts to tie on the eighteenth hole. They both missed and Nicklaus won the championship. That's probably the best finish I've ever seen there.

U.S. Open, Oakmont Country Club, Pittsburgh, 1983

A golf friend told a few stories about trips taken, including this one to the U.S. Open at Oakmont.

A group of us was lucky enough to be entertained by a member at Oakmont, and we arrived on Friday evening the week before the 1983 U.S. Open. We had the last two tee times on Saturday before they closed the course to the public and the members. The track was so difficult when we played it, and the rough was cut after we played. We had some very good golfers in the group, so you can imagine the wagering done the night before we played and the howls of laughter by our host member, who absolutely knew the course would take us to our knees. The scores don't matter, but suffice it to say we were definitely home-towned in a very friendly sort of way, and we didn't even care because it was such a terrific experience. We had caddies who had been there for thirty years, we had our meals in that fine old clubhouse, we played cards, we spent some bucks in the golf shop that was then, and still is, run by University of Tampa graduate Bob Ford.

We watched Tom Watson practice past dusk, alone on the huge practice green (which actually is part of the ninth green), with his wife quietly sitting on the ground nearby. We had dinner one evening with Hal Sutton, then in his rookie year. Did we have fun that weekend! Now when we see a story about Oakmont or hear about fast Open greens, or if we want to conjure an image of what it takes to play professional golf, we remember that time in Pittsburgh and just smile. A couple of the business relationships in the group that were thriving at that time have since drifted apart, but the memory of the weekend at a U.S. Open course, played in tournament condition, with good friends and business associates, will never go away. Fortunately, most of the relationships are still very much intact, and were certainly enhanced by that experience.

24

Etiquette at Professional Golf Tournaments

L et's talk about etiquette when attending any golf tournament. With the added public attention golf has received, there is a new group of spectators. While this is good for the game, it brings with it a double-edged wedge. On one side of the wedge, thousands of new spectators are enjoying the thrill of watching the professionals play. On the other side of the wedge, many of these same spectators have little knowledge of the game, its history, and the etiquette that makes golf such a wonderful spectator sport. As a result, the ever-increasing number of spectators creates additional problems for the players and the fans alike. Here are a few examples of inappropriate behavior:

- Talking, laughing, or making noise during a player's swing

- Yelling too loud after a good shot

- Wearing golf shoes as a spectator (They make noise, unless you have the new soft spikes.)

- Picking up a ball that was hit out-of-bounds

- Walking in nondesignated areas

- Talking to the players when it may break their concentration

- Moving around while a player prepares to hit, or moving to the next tee before the whole group finishes putting out

- Drinking too much alcohol

- Seeking a better place to see the action at the cost of others
- Littering
- Trying to get autographs while the players are on the course

It would seem that this sort of behavior should not be a problem, but we have to remember that many of the new golf spectators are accustomed to relatively rowdy behavior from other sporting events. During a professional golf tournament fans can get unusually close to the players, and without appropriate etiquette and guidelines they can make the players very uncomfortable, if not fearful. As the crowds get bigger, so does the potential for player problems.

Golf was founded on the principle of courtesy to others. It is steeped in tradition and, as BusinessLinksers, we are obligated to preserve golf's rich traditions and help educate newcomers to the sport, course, and game.

Pine Valley, New Jersey, 1985

This outing, described by another golf buddy, ranks as one of his favorite trips.

We were hosted by a couple of members, one of whom was a former CEO of a Fortune 500 company. He was long retired, had been a Pine Valley member for many years, took great pains to line up all the little details months in advance, and periodically updated us on changes that were made in the attendees, including the flight changes! He knew how special it was to play at Pine Valley, and he did everything to make it a wonderful experience for us all. Each of us was given a copy of a book about Pine Valley, and inside the cover, being safely kept as part of the memory, are the letters he wrote to us about our itinerary, hand-pecked on some old Remington typewriter. This was when we first appreciated the idea of giving a guest some memento, whether it be a book, shirt, picture, or something that will last beyond the next round.

We were there for two nights and three days, stayed on the grounds in the "dorms," ate all of our meals in the clubhouse, and spent hours in the extensive upstairs library, where it seemed every golf book known to man is available. There were many autographed copies that had been left there by famous golfers, gifts I suppose, to the club and to the guests who took time to enjoy the ambience of the place. I recall there was a buzzer on the wall to summon the bar for a toddy, and I recall hitting the buzzer too many times. Here, too, we enjoyed the experience of knowledgeable caddies, and we were not bothered by a terrible rainstorm one afternoon; it just gave us an opportunity to rest from one of the toughest golf courses in the world.

The Masters, Augusta National

An annual trip to the mecca of golf has undoubtedly been a highlight each year for these coauthors and friends, all in a strictly business setting.

One year we had three houses rented for the week, so we had many guests, which we dubbed the A team, the B team, and then we had some who just decided it was too much fun, so they were on both teams! It is difficult, to say the least, to procure tickets, but until very recently, it was easy to simply walk up to the gate for the practice rounds, including the famous Par 3 Tournament. So we were up early Monday morning and enjoyed three days of Augusta before the tournament started. Seldom did anyone stay more than one or two nights, so it was just a lot of guys watching a lot of golf with a lot of laughing, with business relationships again being helped along by simply being together at the Mecca of golf. Inevitably, we would get a few tickets for the tournament itself, but to tell you the truth, that became secondary, because the Monday through Wednesday activities were about all we could take.

Fred Ridley won the U.S. Amateur in 1975, was Walker Cup team captain twice, and now practices law in Tampa. He also serves on the executive committee of the USGA. One of his perks as a former U.S. Amateur champion is that he can play in the practice rounds at the Masters. When the rules were changed to allow the golfers to bring their own caddies, somebody had to tote the bag. Well, it was a tough job, but a memory that will rank as tops for the lucky caddies from Tampa. Tuesday and Wednesday duties, including the Par 3 Tournament, were shared by two of us. Having almost as much fun was the rest of the contingent following the foursomes.

It must have appeared that we were having fun, golfers and spectators alike, because a few months later some photographs were sent to Tampa, taken by a lady from North Carolina who wanted us to know that she enjoyed all of us so much that she had to send us these pictures. It turned out that she saw the group, which included television announcer and golf professional Gary Koch, his agent Vinnie Giles (another former U.S. Amateur champion), and Hal Sutton, along with this motley bunch of business associates, and she thought this was a good foursome to follow for the day. We still have the pictures, the memory—and occasionally the same sore back. Those hills are tough.

Another good memory from Augusta, and another year, is ordering lobster from Boston, having it sent directly to the house we rented, and cooking dinner for about fifteen guys. We would all agree on a team to go to the store, somebody would do the salad, somebody cooked the steaks and lobster, one crazy physician took charge of the music (until about 4 A.M.), and somebody else handled dessert (fresh fruit soaked in Grand Marnier over vanilla ice cream).

This may sound like the typical Saturday afternoon in the neighborhood, but it really had the makings of a fraternity function, although with much more plush accommodations. The televisions showed either the tournament highlights from prior years or the latest infomercial on golf equipment, and dinner was enjoyed by golfers who then had to suffer through the Final Four tournament, which happened to be televised the same week.

The houses normally included a housekeeper who came in

the morning, just like at a hotel, so when we returned from the course in the afternoon we could start all over again. You see, that's why a person can only take a day or two of Augusta. The body must relax, and it is not easy when you have a bunch of good friends and business associates, thrilled to be at one of golf's finest events, anxious to tell yet another golf story. We have albums full of pictures, and each year they bring chuckles when we remember all the stories we heard or witnessed. BusinessLinks comes in many forms, but bonding relationships is the key. Can't think of a better venue to make that happen.

The Greatest Shot Ever Witnessed by Pat Summerall

The greatest shot I've ever seen was by Hale Irwin in a playoff at Pebble Beach in 1984. He drove the ball poorly in a bunker on sixteen, popped it up into the bunker. I was working with Tom Weiskopf and Venturi at the time, and Weiskopf said there was no way he could ever get the ball on the green from where he was in that bunker. That day I learned you don't say that, you don't say there is no way, because these guys can do it. It landed on the green and he won the playoff and the tournament. That same day he bounced a ball off the rocks at eighteen back onto the fairway.

25

Charity Tournaments

Charity Tournaments Get Help From Pat

I had my own tournament recently for the Tarrant County (Fort Worth) Council on Alcohol and Drug Abuse. We've had it for three or four years. It's not a big deal, but the cause is certainly worthwhile and we raised $40,000 at our last function. It's a great fund-raising mechanism. I know that's where a lot of networking is done, and it makes sense to stay involved. Fun and sun and money too! A few years back, no one would have dreamed that this fun game of golf could have such an impact on local charities. Today, millions are being raised for all types of worthy causes. Civic clubs, cancer and health associations, universities and the like all use golf tournaments to raise funds to support their programs. Pro-amateur events held prior to PGA and LPGA tournaments are popular and attract local sponsors who are willing to pay big dollars to have their company logo and names displayed and to play in a foursome with a favorite professional golfer or celebrity. The well-planned and promoted tournament can net $20,000 to $100,000, and even more for the big events.

Getting involved in a charity tournament can be fun and good for business. The contacts and friends made are invaluable and generally long lasting, especially those you work with on annual tournaments. Committee assignments mean time spent at these events throughout the year, with opportunities to get to know all kinds of volunteers. The chance to make new friends in a casual atmosphere benefits companies far beyond the event itself. These activities are a must for golfers who can take the time. If a charity or business is considering conducting a golf event for fund-raising or public relations purposes, some organizational suggestions to consider include:

1. Select committee members who can help solicit sponsors and players. Additional volunteers can assist with the other details.

2. Select a golf course that is well known and that would be accepted by sponsors and enjoyed by the golfers. Check to see if the course will waive greens and cart fees. These are major expenses and will help the bottom line and charity involved. Many country clubs will let organizations use their course on Mondays when it is normally closed to members. Offering to pay for the carts, range balls, and food can help close the deal and secure the course. The purchase of gift certificates for flight prizes in the golf shop can be a factor in helping get the course commitment.

3. Send a brochure, flyer, or letter to potential sponsors and players with information about the charity, tournament dates, time schedule, list of sponsors (if secured early), tournament committee, celebrities invited, entry fee, application form for the names of players and handicap, and a map or directions to the golf course.

4. It is always a plus to have a gift bag to give to participants. Popular items include golf balls, divot tools, tees, golf towels, carryall bags, and bag tags. The more expensive tournaments usually throw in a nice jacket, sweater, or golf shoes.

5. The club professional and staff are usually quite willing to assist with many on-course details. Items to be handled include the placement of names on the golf carts, providing markers for long-drive and closest-to-the-pin contests, the announcement of tournament format and special rules prior to tee-off, and tournament scoring to determine the champion or flight winners.

What every ongoing committee likes to hear are comments by the sponsors, golfers, and volunteers that their event was one of the best, most profitable, and well-run tournaments in the area. Whether it's fun raising or fund-raising, you can't beat golf!

26

The Tour Professionals

> I would say that many tour professionals don't know how
> to effectively use golf as a business tool.
>
> —Twenty-five-year tour veteran

rofessional golfers have an extraordinary opportunity to
develop business relationships. Everyone wants to play
with a golfer with unique talents, and they all can play the
game. Being able to watch pros shape the shot, based on the conditions, or make one long putt after another is always a thrill to
the amateur. Professional golfers have enormous opportunities to
use the game as a business development tool. Surprisingly, we
have found that many professional players neglect the opportunity. We talked with many professionals and, let's face it, they
are all deeply imbedded with the time constraints of a week-to-
week schedule that is often just a series of highs and lows. If it's
been a good week at the last event, the pro-am partners can feel
it in the way the professional sets the tone on the first tee. If it is
an obligatory pro-am round the amateurs know it, feel it, and
frankly, often resent it. Perhaps they resent it more than the professional does. This is a real job to a professional, and it's an
outing for the amateurs, who often pay dearly for the privilege.

As amateurs, we should be respectful of the professional's
time and not take advantage of it. We are not there for a lesson;
we are there to enjoy an experience we hope we can talk about
for a long time.

Nevertheless, here is what we observed time and again in the
pro-ams. The discussions are among the amateurs, with the pro-

fessional keeping to himself, rather than enjoying the camaraderie. Instead of getting to know the amateurs, who may have opportunities down the road for the golf professional (through outings, sponsorships, and referrals, all important parts of a career income), the pro's concentration is only on the course and the score. We don't want to make any generalizations, but we do think that the professionals could loosen up a bit more sometimes.

BusinessLinks Without Taking a Swing

There are other ways to develop business relationships through golf without having to play. One of the most powerful tools is to offer a two- to three-hour golf clinic to a specified market. A simple one-page mailer-invitation can be sent to a thousand or so individuals, inviting them to your golf clinic. You can expect twenty-five to fifty people to attend. But it works even better, and more effectively, if the invitations are very special, say, to just a few existing relationships as opposed to a blanket mailing.

All you need to do is pick a club that has a driving range and banquet facility for up to fifty golfers. Negotiate with two of the local teaching pros to provide two hours of instruction to the group on a specific aspect of the game. The two professionals can teach simultaneously at opposite ends of the range. Plan the event on a Saturday and mail your invitations thirty days in advance of the event.

Your invitations should highlight the PGA professionals who will be teaching and the purpose of the offer. Indicate that your company is sponsoring this event. Typically, a nominal charge is appropriate, especially if the professionals have one of the many "swing analysis" techniques available as part of the package. Golfers are always looking for a new way to help their games, and the high-tech tools now available are both valuable and effective.

At the clubhouse, have a continental breakfast set up and be prepared to speak for no more than a few minutes. Let the groups know you are trying to develop a personal relationship with them, and this is one way to do so. That's all. Nothing gets sold. The group is there for golf, at your invitation. Lay out the program, then sit back and let the professionals do what they do best.

Then it's off to the driving range and splitting the golfers into two groups, so each professional has a small number to work with. If swing analysis is available, your guest will have something to take home, and you have something to follow up on. The purpose is to have your guests spend some time with golf professionals, gaining some insight on the skills of the game. You have their business cards, and also an event you have shared, hopefully one that was done first class. Now you have a reason to talk about business, as long as the guest feels the day was an enjoyable experience.

Respect the Professionals' "Office Time"

We all know that pro-am events are also very needed practice rounds for the tournament, but a touch of "lighten up" is all that most amateurs need to see in the professional to make amateurs feel much more part of the outing, and the experience. (The practice tee following the round is the golf professional's "office environment," and is usually a time during the day when the golfer really does not want to be disturbed. This is most definitely something that amateurs should be aware of.)

The caddie could often be more open with the amateurs and not affect his ability to take care of the pro in any way. By the way, caddies who are cognizant of the amateurs in those pro-ams deserve a nice tip, and that, too, is often not handled well by amateurs. The caddie appreciates gratuities, and while this is not an absolute requirement, based on many years of pro-am experience, BusinessLinks thinks it should be.

Mental and Physical, It's All Fun to Watch

There are competing views as to what is the most difficult part of golf. Some say it's the physical side of the game, while others say it's the mental aspect. One might argue that the physical part is more difficult because it takes so much time and practice to groove the stroke. Others contend that many sports are a great deal more physically demanding, such as tennis at the professional level, or football. Our discussions with professional golfers found that they believed the hardest part of the game is the mental side. We can see that in the pro-am experience, where heavy concentration finds a few birdies with seemingly effortless swings, and the calculated execution of shots we can't begin to think about, much less pull out of our own bag.

Shooting a Low Score Doesn't Mean You'll Get the Business

Throughout this entire book we have focused on the amateur's mental side of golf communication skills, personalities, and attitudes. While professional golfers may have tremendous physical skills and mental concentration, they, too, must learn to master the interpersonal skills essential for the development of business relationships.

What we found is that many professional golfers are so focused on scoring that, when they have an opportunity to network for business on the course, they lose sight of the potential relationship that is literally waiting to fall in their lap. Many professional golfers believe that the most important thing they can do in the amateur setting is to impress their playing partners with a great score. The concentration seems too focused on scoring, while showing other golfers a good time is way down in the line of importance. Again, it is the balance of effort in each of these areas which creates the experience for all concerned.

Gary Koch and Peter Jacobson are two tour players who have mastered the task of making amateurs appreciate the experience of playing with an accomplished and matured golf professional. They have fun throughout the round, know when to tell a joke or two, when to give a serious golf tip, and, most of all, how to say thanks to the amateurs. They are a class act, and their actions go a long way toward building public goodwill—which translates to business opportunities. Not surprisingly, both of these professionals have built an enormous backlog of business relationships and continue to enjoy the fruits of career seeds planted long ago. Their personal relationships with other professionals have translated into many a favor being done, and their own careers continue to be enhanced along the way.

Obviously, there are other professional golfers who are excellent at building business relationships while playing the game. We are by no means denigrating the abilities of golf's masters. We seek to point out what may appear to be obvious, but which in our research begs to be reiterated. We see successes every week, but only a small percentage of those are "on tour." Many have made it on tour financially, while others have not. Some are in and out of "Tour School" several times over their career. It is those who understand the power of personal-relationship building who will make it in the business world outside of the tour. They will use golf as a stepping-stone to get what they want and deserve in the business world.

We have had the pleasure of playing golf with a few sports psychologists who focus on professional golfers, and much of their counseling deals with mind control and preparation: how to control anger; how to stay focused; how to get in a routine before every shot. Of course, there are many other aspects they deal with, such as family communication and support. But, overwhelmingly, the psychologists we interviewed confirmed the fact that most professional golfers, when playing golf for business purposes, focus too much on scoring rather than the art of building business relationships.

It does not matter whether you are an amateur or a professional golfer when it comes to BusinessLinks. What matters is your ability to enjoy the game with your playing partners, as it was meant to be enjoyed.

Mulligan

- Make sure the guest you invite to play in a charity tournament can carry himself in the game.

- Charity involvement is for golfers and nongolfers alike.

- There is more than one way to use golf as a business development tool.

- Play for fun and enjoy the experience.

- Respect professional golfers' time during and after the rounds.

Postround Closing Comments

As you have read this book, we hope that you have picked up a few ideas to place in your business golf bag. Our message has been simple: BusinessLinks is the next major development in golf. We believe it is quite possibly the most important element in the game today. It's learning how to enjoy the game at any level by preserving its traditions and etiquette. It's about mastering personal course management strategies and personal communication skills so that you can develop an all-important relationship for business, political, or personal gain. It's enjoying the game with whomever you choose to play, whatever their skill level. Remember, BusinessLinks isn't about scoring, it's not about how well you hit the ball, or how far you hit it. It's about showing your character, honesty, and humor in order to develop a bond with playing partners that can last a lifetime. It's how to plan it, how to work it, and, most important, how to follow up. BusinessLinks is a sophisticated understanding of what some golfers have been doing successfully for a long time.

Golf can bring out the best and the worst in all of us. If played in the spirit that it was originally meant, how can we not profit from each and every time we play it? Allow golf to enhance your life and enrich your relationships.

> A keen ear to listen with
>   will always make 'em smile;
> A little bit of courtesy will bring 'em in a mile;
> A little bit of friendliness
>   will tickle 'em, it's plain—
> And a solid round of BusinessLinks
>   will bring 'em back again.

Afterword

Business Golf was created after a national survey was conducted by the authors. The survey was targeted at top CEOs from all over the country with two primary questions being asked:

1. Does the CEO know how employees represent the company on the golf course?

2. Does the CEO know what the return on investment is regarding company golf, or is the CEO able to track the efforts of employees for accountability purposes?

Unanimously, the answers were "No." Hence this book and the development of BusinessLinks International, Inc., a Tampa, Florida, company determined to help golfers of all levels be more effective using golf for business purposes.

BusinessLinks International, Inc., also provides education through entertaining and sophisticated seminar events, and offers situational experience for corporations and individuals in several formats. Each BusinessLinks event is not only a unique learning experience for participants, it is also used as an effective marketing and client service opportunity for organizations. Each seminar event is unique, entertaining, interactive, and, most important, educational. *Our goal is to dispel the myth that only good golfers can effectively use golf as a business development tool, and to expose the areas where many good golfers fail.* Being competitive in today's business environment requires learning new skills, one of which is golf. Upper management and sales and marketing staffs need to be consistent in their corporate image, and accountability is only prudent business. BusinessLinks provides the ultimate learning and networking experience to accomplish those goals.

For additional information on BusinessLinks, contact the authors at: *buslinks@gate.net*

About the Authors

Pat Summerall was the signature voice of the CBS golf team from 1968 to 1994, during which time he covered the eighteenth hole of the Masters. Today, he is still considered the premier golf sportscaster. Summerall began his broadcasting career with CBS in 1961. Since that time, he has worked twenty-seven Super Bowls on network television, including Superbowl XVI, the highest rated sports program of all time. In addition to football and golf, Summerall broadcast several U.S. Open tennis championships, beginning in 1971. He has had the good fortune to have played golf with some of the most prominent personalities in the game. They include presidents, commissioners, sports stars, actors, and CEOs of Fortune 500 companies.

Will D. Rhame has spent his career as a financial and marketing consultant, focusing his energies on developing unique marketing concepts for individuals and companies. He is responsible for the original idea behind this book and BusinessLinks International, Inc., the cofounder of BusinessLinks International, Inc., and directs the company's training programs. Rhame is the founder of the CPA Club, the largest national franchise of its kind, designed as a premier networking organization for professionals. Although golf is his passion, he is also an avid tennis player. Rhame moved to Florida in 1992 from San Diego with his wife, Debbie, and their three children.

Jim McNulty, CPA, has practiced accounting since 1971, and at age twenty-six began his own accounting firm, which grew to be one of Florida's largest. He has played golf competitively and socially since he was seven years old, and consistently uses the game to nurture and expand relationships. He is cofounder of

BusinessLinks International, Inc., and currently lives in Richmond, Virginia, with his wife, Dora. His daughter and one son are recent college graduates, while their two other sons are in their final years of college. He is the CFO of Star Scientific, Inc., and a consultant to several entrepreneurial companies.